ORIGIN
OF THE
SOUL

AND THE PURPOSE OF
REINCARNATION

Expanded Edition with Past Lives of Jesus

by
WALTER SEMKIW, MD

Dedicated to Svetka,
for her love and support

Table of Contents

Reincarnation Case List

Amorite King of Jerusalem   King Herod   Adolph Hitler
Amorite King of Hebron   Roman Senator   Joseph Goebbels
Amorite King of Eglon   Son of King Herod   Benito Mussolini
Amorite King of Lachish   Judas
Amorite King of Jarmuth   Roman General   Joseph Stalin

Dipole Case List

Moshe Dyan   Anwar Sadat
Benedict Arnold   George Washington
Muhammad Ali   Joe Frasier
Mahatma Gandhi   Nehru
Christopher Marlow   William Shakespeare
Thomas Edison   Henry Ford
Oliver Hardy   Stan Laurel
John Lennon   Paul McCartney
Robert Koch   Louis Pasteur
Charles Darwin   Jean Baptist Lamarck
St. Clare of Assisi   St. Francis of Assisi
St. John of the Cross St. Teresa of Avila
Jesus   Mary, Mother of Jesus
Alexander Hamilton   James Madison
John Adams   Thomas Jefferson

1

Introduction and www.ReincarnationResearch.com: Establishing a Science of Spirituality

In my previous books, *Born Again* and *Return of the Revolutionaries,* cases were compiled and presented which demonstrate objective evidence of reincarnation. It is my belief that evidence of reincarnation will lead to a science of spirituality, which in turn will help humanity evolve much more quickly and peacefully.

Two categories of reincarnation cases have been featured in my books. One involves cases that are independently researched or derived, such as those studied by Ian Stevenson, MD at the University of Virginia, and the independently derived cases of Robert Snow, Jeff Keene, Norm Shealy, Barbro Karlen and others.

The second category involves cases derived through the work that I have been doing with Kevin Ryerson, a trance medium who is featured in three of Shirley MacLaine's books, including *Out on a Limb.* When functioning as a trance medium, Kevin goes into a meditative state and allows selected spirit beings to utilize his body to communicate with human beings. When this occurs, Kevin has no awareness or memory of what these spirit guides are saying.

Since 2001, I have worked with a particular spirit guide channeled through Kevin named Ahtun Re, who has demonstrated the ability to make what appear to be accurate past-life matches. In particular, the reincarnation cases of Ralph Nader, Carl Sagan, Neale

Donald Walsch and Oprah Winfrey, which are featured in *Born Again* and *Return of the Revolutionaries,* dramatically demonstrate Ahtun Re's gift for conveying past life information. The reincarnation cases involving Laurel & Hardy, featured in *Born Again*, also show Ahtun Re's uncanny ability to determine accurate matches.

Ahtun Re is a soul who has experienced a cycle of evolution on Earth, but who has chosen not to reincarnate since about 1350 BC. Instead, he has for more than three thousand years observed humanity develop from the vantage point of the spiritual world.

If someone had told me a few years ago that I would write a book in collaboration with a trance medium and an Egyptian spirit guide, I would have thought that quite far-fetched. However, in working with Kevin for over a decade and having had one to two sessions with him each month, I have come to the conclusion that Ahtun Re is a spirit being separate from Kevin's own soul who has access to what some term Universal Mind and others call the Akashic Records.

It is Ahtun Re's ability to tap into this source of information that allows him to solve reincarnation cases accurately. Because of this ability, I find him to be a valuable research partner, who is also very good-hearted. In addition, I have found Kevin himself to be a wonderful friend. He is honest and ethical, and he also has a brilliant mind. In allowing spirit guides like Ahtun Re to communicate with humanity, Kevin is providing a unique service. I, like many others, consider him to be the world's pre-eminent trance medium and I have often called him the Edgar Cayce of our time.

In *Born Again* and *Return of the Revolutionaries,* I have compiled reincarnation cases that demonstrate objective evidence of reincarnation not only in an effort to provide proof that reincarnation exists, but also to define patterns and characteristics that demonstrate how it works. Objective evidence of reincarnation will grow over time as more people remember past lives that can be historically verified, or discover them through other means. Due to the Internet and mass media, evidence of reincarnation will increasingly be distributed around the world.

If we accept that reincarnation is real, questions naturally follow that center on the purpose of reincarnation and the nature of the spirit world. Unfortunately, most of us cannot perceive the spirit world. In an effort to address the purpose of reincarnation, we must rely on people who have special gifts such as clairvoyance. In addition, we can solicit the testimony of inhabitants of the spirit world themselves, like Ahtun Re and other spirit guides channeled through Kevin Ryerson, including Tom MacPherson, an Irish guide who will be introduced later, and another called John.

Kevin's guide John provides us with a unique opportunity to understand the New Testament of Christianity. He identifies himself as an Essene, a disciple of Jesus, and in fact as the Apostle John, who wrote the Gospel of John. Communications from John can be studied in depth in Kevin's book, *Spirit Communication: The Soul's Path.* Indeed, transcriptions of John's messages in *Spirit Communication* form an updated version of the Gospel of John, with even linguistic similarities evident. I thank Kevin for allowing me to use information from his book.

In the pages that follow, several concepts from the Bible will be examined in relation to soul evolution. Because Kevin Ryerson's guide John has identified himself as the Apostle John, more attention is given to Judeo-Christian concepts than to those of other theologies. In addition, Ahtun Re has revealed that he served as a spirit guide to Jesus during his incarnation which led to the crucifixion and resurrection. I myself was raised in the United States by Catholic parents, so my primary religious exposure has been to Judeo-Christian concepts. I regret that other theologies are not given equal time in the chapters that follow. I hope that this shortcoming can be rectified in subsequent publications.

Others whom I have asked to contribute to this book, individuals who have gifts of clairvoyance and who have had direct experience with the spirit world and spirit beings, are listed below. I have provided their websites, as well as Kevin Ryerson's, for those who would like to learn more about them and their work.

Echo Bodine	www.echobodine.com
Judy Goodman	www.judygoodman.com
Kevin Ryerson	www.kevinryerson.com
Michael Tamura	www.michaeltamura.com

I have also drawn ideas from various sources such as Theosophy and the works of Alice Bailey to help understand the purpose of reincarnation. Before including material from any source, I have consulted Ahtun Re to determine whether the concepts are valid. As such, information in this book has the seal of approval from at least one inhabitant of the spiritual planes, a spirit being who has demonstrated an aptitude for making reincarnation matches that can be factually validated. Ahtun Re is thus a guiding light for *Origin of the Soul and the Purpose of Reincarnation.*

I would also like to point out that I consider material presented in this book to be a starting point. As time goes by, others will emerge who will be able to experience the spirit realms and who will contribute new discoveries and developments. We have created an organization called the Institute for the Integration of Science, Intuition and Spirit that is dedicated to reincarnation research and the study of spiritual realms. Our website is www. ReincarnationResearch.com. We hope to establish a world-wide network that will serve to collect, analyze and archive reincarnation cases.

In addition, we are dedicated to catalyzing the positive societal change that objective evidence of reincarnation can bring, as this evidence demonstrates that individuals can change religious, national and ethnic affiliation from one incarnation to another. It is our sincere hope and expectation that as this research is disseminated, conflicts based on differences in religion, race, nationality and ethnic origin will be mitigated.

We need your help to accomplish these goals. To create a more peaceful world, evidence of reincarnation must be available to people of all cultures and in multiple languages. Our website is equipped with Google Translate, which means that our case studies are available in 104 languages. Participate in making the world a better place by letting your friends and associates know about our site:

www.ReincarnationResearch.com

2

Creation of the Universe and of Souls

The Big Bang and Creation of the Physical Universe

According to Ahtun Re, the story of creation is described fairly accurately in the Gospel of John. I will relate this story with clarifications from Ahtun Re and John himself, as found in Kevin Ryerson's book, *Spirit Communication: The Soul's Path.* As mentioned, the spirit guide that Kevin channels, who speaks in a whispery, hushed voice and who calls himself John, has identified himself as the Apostle John, who is also the author of the Gospel of John.

The Creation of the Physical Universe, Monads, Souls and Dipoles

According to John and Ahtun Re, God created the physical universe in the Big Bang, which scientists estimate occurred about 14 billion years ago. God did this as a creative act and the physical universe can be considered to be the body of God.

Ahtun Re relates that God created souls associated with our universe "a nanosecond" after the Big Bang. We can image that souls were split off as little fragments of God, little pieces of God budding from God. I asked Ahtun Re, "Why did God create souls?" He responded, "God created the universe and souls as God wanted to express oneness through diversity. God wanted to express diversity."

I also asked Ahtun Re whether there are other Gods who have created other universes through other Big Bangs – universes which exist, perhaps, in other dimensions. Ahtun Re told me that there is only one God.

As described in *Spirit Communication* and affirmed by Ahtun Re, God created all souls associated with this universe at the same time. I asked Ahtun Re what existed before the Big Bang. He stated that there was "nothingness, pure consciousness." Ahtun Re then added that God himself had prior manifestations and that there was a universe that existed prior to our universe, prior to the Big Bang estimated to have occurred 14 billion years ago. Souls who existed in this prior universe continued to exist following our Big Bang. So, although the physical structure of the universe is destroyed and recreated though the phenomenon of Big Bangs, souls endure.

Ahtun Re explained that a small number of souls that existed before our Big Bang agreed to incarnate into our current universe. I asked Ahtun Re whether these souls brought with them abilities, talents and gifts from their prior existences. He said that they did and that great leaders of humanity like the Buddha, Moses, Jesus, Mohammed, Krishna and others existed prior to the creation of our universe. They and thousands of others agreed to incarnate once again into physical existence to lead and serve humanity. These experienced souls entered physical existence through the same portal as new souls did, a nanosecond after the Big Bang, 14 billion years ago.

The Monad, the Soul and Our Energy Spectrum

When God created us, we were imbued with specific qualities that remain with us throughout our existence. This is why, through various incarnations, we tend to demonstrate similar character traits, passions and talents. In *Born Again,* we observed that Paul Gauguin has reincarnated again as an artist, in the persona of Peter Teekamp. Similarly, Pablo Picasso has reincarnated as the artist Alexandra Nechita.

General Daniel Morgan, a military hero in the American Revolution, has reincarnated as George W. Bush, a political leader with a tendency to address problems with military force. American Civil War General John B. Gordon has reincarnated as Assistant Fire

Chief Jeff Keene, who notes that serving in a fire department approximates serving in the military in terms of dealing with danger and the structure of ranks. Laurel & Hardy have once again reincarnated as comedians, the Bacher Boys.

To better understand our qualities of personality and our spiritual evolution, we will differentiate between the monad and the soul. We will use the term "monad" to describe that part of our spiritual anatomy which remains in union with God, which remains on the plane of existence that is the home of God's consciousness. If we bud from God, the monad can be considered the bud that remains on the vine that is God. The monad can be considered identical to "spirit."

We will define the "soul" as a projection of the monad that travels through various other dimensions or planes, usually described as "lower" relative to the plane where the monad, or spirit, resides. The soul travels to these lower dimensions or planes to gain experience and to establish identity. The soul is the repository of our experiences across lifetimes.

The ancient Egyptians believed in reincarnation and they too divided one's spiritual anatomy into parts, most notably the "Ba" and the "Ka." Though the Egyptians' understanding of the Ba and Ka is somewhat different, Ahtun Re has indicated that for our purposes, we can view the Ba as the equivalent of the monad and the Ka as akin to the soul.

I asked Ahtun Re whether the monad and soul were created at the same time. He stated that they were created simultaneously. He also confirmed that the template for our facial appearance was also created at the same time as the monad and the soul were created, and that this template is a mathematical property of the soul. One's particular facial template may be perceived as beautiful or unattractive in different incarnations, based on physical attributes governing a particular incarnation, such as the condition of the face and teeth, body weight, etc. Social mores, what society deems as fashionable, will also influence whether one is perceived as attractive or unattractive. Though we maintain the same bone structure, the same basic facial appearance, we can take turns, from lifetime to lifetime, of being perceived as beautiful or plain.

We will use the analogy of a yo-yo, the toy that is held in the hand, rolls down a string and then rebounds into the hand, to explain the relationship between our monad or spirit and our soul. Imagine that the monad is the point where the string of the yo-yo attaches to the hand, or perhaps imagine the monad as the hand itself. The yo-yo is anchored in the monad in the plane that is the home of God. The monad is like an appendage extending from God, part of God and yet having its own existence.

Although the yo-yo, the soul, travels away from God to lower dimensions, it is always connected to the monad by its string. In Hindu philosophy, there is even a term, the "antakarana," to describe this energetic link, the string that runs between the monad and the soul. In the West, the antakarana has also been called the "rainbow bridge."

Now that we have made a distinction between the monad and soul, let us describe how we were created with unique characteristics. Let us image that the monad, the spark of our existence that derives from God, is like a prism that diffracts white light. When we think of a prism, we usually imagine it as triangular in shape and we see seven colors emanating from it, the seven colors of the visible spectrum.

Let us imagine that when we, as monads, were created, we each were endowed with our own unique prism that gives off a combination of colors or energies that characterizes us. Some monads produce an energy spectrum that has red as a predominant color, other monads produce primarily green, and others yellow or blue. We will call this unique spectrum our "energy signature" or "energy spectrum."

In our analogy of the yo-yo, the monad, our prism, produces a characteristic spectrum of light and transmits this light to our soul, the round body of the yo-yo. When we incarnate into a physical body, our soul in turn transmits our energy spectrum into us. Imagine that the soul is able to project a hologram, a three-dimensional image, into the developing physical body. This energy hologram includes the template that our bones and tissues grow around, which results in our characteristic appearance, and our facial architecture in particular. The hologram also transmits our energy spectrum, which is then reflected in our character traits, aptitudes and interests.

Your soul, then, is a dynamic energy structure that oversees and animates your incarnation. You are a holographic projection of your soul in a physical body. Your soul, however, is more than you, for you are your soul in only one focal point of time and space. Your soul is you, but your soul is also the sum of all the incarnations it has had. Most of us do not have a conscious connection with our soul, but some do, as evidenced by recollections of past lives. One of the features of spiritual advancement is a more conscious connection with our soul.

At this point, let us delve into ways in which we can better understand our energy spectrums, the unique set of energies or colors that make us who we are.

3

The Seven Rays

One model of personality that I would like to use to better illustrate the nature of the soul is called the "Seven Rays," as described in Theosophical literature. I refer to this model as it fits nicely with the concept of each of us having an energy signature or energy spectrum consisting of a combination of colors. The Seven Rays, though, is only one model and we will also discuss other systems that can be used to understand our energy spectrum.

I will use historical figures to illustrate the various ray types. These categorizations have been drawn from writers such as Alice Bailey and Benjamin Creme, as well as from Ahtun Re. I am aware that different sources may classify individuals in slightly different ways.

We can understand these classification differences in that we are not only of one ray type. Rather, we are all like fountains with seven jets that emit the energy of the seven rays in different proportions. Some of us emit primarily one ray, some a combination of rays. The key thing to understand is that we have a unique energy signature, an energy spectrum that is our own, which is manifest from one incarnation to another. The Seven Rays are sketched as follows:

First Ray: the energy of will, which produces a focus on power and exerting influence

Individuals who have energy signatures with a great deal of First Ray energy are attracted to leadership positions in government, the military, corporate structures, etc. First Ray individuals like action and they enjoy action-oriented professions like police work and firefighting. Athletes demonstrate the energy of will. Historical examples of First Ray types include Alexander the Great, Indira Gandhi, Leonid Brezhnev, Joseph Stalin and Nikita Khrushchev.

First Ray types are often distinguished by great courage, but they can also cause great destruction. This may be of benefit if outdated organizations and forms undergo renewal thereby, but destruction usually wastes resources and infrastructure. Ultimately, conflict is unnecessary and humanity will leap forward in evolutionary terms when First Ray types focus their leadership skills on building rather than destroying. Indeed, more evolved First Ray types will increasingly gravitate towards leadership roles in government and corporations rather than in the military.

One example of an individual who has been associated with First Ray energy is the French Emperor Napoleon, who conquered many lands, but also created great destruction and suffering. Though this case needs further evaluation, Napoleon has been identified, through the work that I have done with Kevin Ryerson and Ahtun Re, as having reincarnated as Jack Welch, the former Chief Executive Officer of General Electric, who transformed GE from a household appliance manufacturer to a multinational, diversified corporation.

Welch, like Napoleon, has been an outstanding leader who greatly expanded his domain over the course of his career. In contemporary times, Welch expressed his First Ray qualities in the boardroom instead of on the battlefield. This is a more highly evolved expression of leadership skills and Ahtun Re predicts that Welch will reincarnate in the future to create corporations of great benevolence.

Misuse of First Ray energy can be seen as the cause of most violence and crime, in that one person's will is imposed on another person inappropriately. Unfortunately, through mass media, the expression of will over others is glorified in action and horror movies. Being a "Terminator" has become glamorous, which likely encourages misuse of First Ray energy in tragic ways, such as in school shootings.

More attention will be spent on First Ray issues than on those pertaining to the other rays as it is this energy that causes the most trouble and creates the most negative karma for individuals and nations. Indeed, "anger management" courses should be integrated into the curricula of schools everywhere so that misuse of First Ray energy is curtailed, not glorified.

Second Ray: the energy of love-wisdom, which produces a desire to better understand the human condition and to uplift humanity

Individuals with energy signatures rich in the Second Ray are dedicated to using wisdom to enhance social order. Souls with Second Ray energy are motivated by the desire to help society at large, with the ultimate aim of ending social injustice and suffering. They are often charismatic, pragmatic individuals who demonstrate empathy: they are the teachers and the social activists of the world. Many times, they produce written works that embody the social conditions of the time.

Historical examples of Second Ray types include Mahatma Gandhi, William Shakespeare, Carl Jung, Lao Tse, Leo Tolstoy, Krishnamurti and Nikolai Gogol. Ahtun Re has suggested that talk show host Oprah Winfrey, former US President Bill Clinton and former Vice-President Al Gore are Second Ray types.

Third Ray: the energy of creative intelligence, which produces a desire to create objects of practical value

Souls marked by Third Ray energy enjoy using science, mathematics and other disciplines in practical applications. They are the engineers and the architects of the world and the creators of technology. Examples from history include Alexander Graham Bell, Madame Curie and Antoine Lavoisier. Ahtun Re has suggested that Thomas Edison and Frank Lloyd Wright were Third Ray types. Economists can be viewed as expressing Third Ray energy. One of the world's most famous economic theorists, Adam Smith, has been confirmed by Ahtun Re to have reincarnated in contemporary times as US economist Jeffrey Sachs, author of *The End of Poverty: Economic Possibilities for Our Time.*

Fourth Ray: the energy of art and beauty

Fourth Ray souls are the artists, musicians and actors of the world. Fourth Ray types from history include Pablo Picasso, Paul Gauguin, Wolfgang Amadeus Mozart, Ludwig van Beethoven, Frederic Chopin, Jimi Hendrix and Louis Armstrong. In contemporary times in India, actors Amitabh Bachchan and Shah Rukh Khan represent Fourth Ray types.

Fourth Ray types also include Hans Christian Andersen and Edvard Grieg, artists who are reincarnated in contemporary times. Hans Christian Andersen was born in 1805 in Denmark. As a boy, he loved to tell stories and used puppets to create dramas. His father built him a miniature theatre, which Hans used to stage puppet plays.

As a young man, Andersen was sensitive and effeminate in nature. His peers teased him and questioned whether Hans was a boy or a girl. After spending his early years in a small town named Odense, he moved to Copenhagen as a young man.

As an adult, Andersen traveled extensively and wrote narratives about his journeys, which become popular travelogues. He went on to write fairy tales and stories, such as *Thumbelina, The Ugly Ducking* and *The Princess and the Pea,* which have become literary classics. Later in life, during one of his trips to England, Andersen stayed with Charles Dickens for several weeks. As described in *Born Again,* Dickens has reincarnated as J. K. Rowling, author of the *Harry Potter* series. Anderson died in 1875.

As confirmed by Ahtun Re, Hans Christian Andersen has reincarnated as Erik Berglund, who is a storyteller and an international recording artist. Erik has noted many similarities between himself and Andersen.

For example, Erik relates that as a young man he was very sensitive and androgynous in nature. Erik grew up in a town named Northfield, in the state of Minnesota, where many Scandinavian immigrants settled in the United States. As a young man, he relocated to New York City. In doing so, Erik replicated a pattern that Andersen demonstrated in moving from a small town to a big city.

It was in 1974, in New York, that Erik stumbled upon a statue of Hans Christian Andersen. In addition to noting a physical resemblance, Erik knew intuitively and with certainty that he was Anderson in a previous incarnation. Eric would keep this information, this inner knowledge regarding Andersen, to himself for another 33 years.

In 1976, at a time when he was confused about his direction in life, Erik met and was befriended by Norman Ernsting and his wife, who took Erik into their home. Erik relates that he and Norman had an instant rapport and that Norman felt Erik was like "family."

Norman had built a puppet theater at the *Children's Museum of the Native American* in New York City. Erik had always had an innate love and talent for telling stories and now he found expression for this gift in creating puppet dramas with Norman. The two entertained hundreds of children on a regular basis with their puppet shows.

While living in New York, Erik learned to play the Irish Harp and eventually he became a recording artist. Like Anderson, Erik has traveled extensively around the world giving concerts. In his performances, harp music is interwoven with storytelling.

I met Erik in 2007 and can attest that as a craftsman of stories, as well as a musician, he is exceptionally gifted. Knowing of my interest in reincarnation, Eric revealed his past-life connection with Andersen. Erik also shared his hypothesis that Norman Ernsting is the reincarnation of the father of Hans Christian Andersen. Recall that Andersen's father build a puppet theater for Hans, much as Norman has done in contemporary times. Also, note that Norman took Erik into his home as a member of his family, something that Norman has never done for any other person.

Subsequently, in a session with Kevin Ryerson, Ahtun Re agreed that Erik Berglund is the reincarnation of Hans Christian Andersen and that Norman Ernsting is the reincarnation of the Anderson's father. Erik is now discussing his reincarnation case in public forums.

It was Erik who told me about Canadian musician Paul Armitage, who, it turned out, believes that he may be the reincarnation of the Norwegian composer, Edvard Grieg. Grieg was born in 1843 and died in 1907.

Paul has written a pamphlet regarding his proposed past-life match as Grieg. In his narrative, Paul explains that he performs as a keyboard artist at many festivals and conferences, including spiritual ones. In addition, he composes unique "Musical Soul Portraits" for clients, which is one of the ways that he earns a living.

In April 2001, a woman with clairvoyant gifts met Paul at a spiritual festival in Mount Shasta, California. After listening to a Musical Soul Portrait that Paul had composed, this psychic, while in a meditative state, wrote down the word "Grieg" on a piece of paper and handed it to Paul.

Paul explains that on many occasions, after his concerts or at spiritual conferences, people have proposed past lives for him. For example, one person told him that he is the reincarnation of Beethoven, another saw him as the reincarnation of Mozart. Paul always innately knew that these proposed past-life matches were untrue. As such, what happened when Paul was given the note with the word Grieg on it was totally unexpected.

Paul relates that when he read the word Grieg, a rush of intense emotional energy ran through his body and that he experienced an otherworldly sense of familiarity. In his narrative, Paul has written that it "was very much like a Déjà vu experience, except there was nothing to 'recall.'" This type of reaction was also experienced by neurosurgeon and inventor of the TENS Unit, Norm Shealy, MD, PhD, when he first heard the name of his past-life persona, John Elliotson, as described in *Return of the Revolutionaries* and *Born Again*.

A few weeks later, when Paul was back home in Vancouver, Canada, he was driving in his car and unintentionally tuned his radio to the classical music station. Though Paul was trained as a classical musician, he rarely listens to this type of music anymore. The piece of music playing on the radio, though, had a profound effect on him. Regarding that moment, Paul has written:

> *I caught a piece of classical music playing on the radio that literally riveted me. I had never heard this piece before, I had no idea what the title was or who was the composer of this music. But I was transfixed and completely caught up in the beauty of this piece as I sat listening in my car. I distinctly recall, as I listened, being very aware of a particular quality in the harmonic movement of this piece, that I totally resonated with as a musician.*

The radio announcer then reported that the music was composed by Edvard Grieg. Though Paul was moved by this experience, he still did not bother to research Grieg. It was only when he was visiting a friend and Paul shared the episodes related to Grieg, that his friend pulled out a music encyclopedia. Paul was startled as he looked at a portrait of Grieg, as Paul bears an uncanny resemblance to him. Not only are facial features remarkably consistent, but Paul, who is still a young man, has the same dramatic, thick, white hair as Grieg. Paul has also noted that Grieg's style of musical composition is very much like his own, an observation that I can attest to having heard compositions of both artists.

Let me now share a story which suggests that spiritual guidance has been in play in Paul's story. While in Europe, through a series of synchronistic events beyond his control, Paul was able to visit the home of Edvard Grieg and while there, he was given special permission to play on Grieg's own grand piano. A picture was taken of this homecoming. In the background of this image, an old photograph is seen on the wall, which features Grieg playing this very same instrument, with his white hair flowing backwards. In the foreground of the contemporary photo, Paul is playing Grieg's piano, with the same facial profile and dramatic hair, producing a mirror image. It is a riveting scene.

In a subsequent session with Kevin Ryerson in 2007, I asked Ahtun Re if Paul is indeed the reincarnation of Grieg. I should point out that Ahtun Re does not automatically confirm proposed past-life matches. Oftentimes, he states that proposed reincarnation matches are incorrect. In working with Ahtun Re over the course of years, my assessment is that his determinations are trustworthy.

In this case, Ahtun Re did confirm that Paul Armitage is the reincarnation of Edvard Grieg. Like Erik Berglund, Paul is now discussing his reincarnation case in public. In addition, Erik and Paul are performing in concerts together. In my opinion, we are blessed to be able to enjoy the talents of Hans Christian Andersen and Edvard Grieg once again. To learn more about Paul Armitage's work, please go to:

www.paularmitagemusic.com

The reincarnation cases involving Erik and Paul have been used to demonstrate how Fourth Ray types replicate artistic patterns across incarnations. Michelangelo is one of the most famous artists in history and one would expect him to be in the category of a Fourth Ray type. It has been suggested by Benjamin Creme that Michelangelo also demonstrates First Ray energy, which is manifest in the grand scale and power that many of Michelangelo's works demonstrate, such as his *David,* the ceiling of the Sistine Chapel and the dome of St. Peter's. It will be proposed that Michelangelo has re-incarnated in contemporary times in the person of Paul-Felix Montez, who is again producing "Big Art." The Michelangelo | Montez case will be discussed in a subsequent chapter on child prodigies.

Fifth Ray: the energy of science, which produces a desire to understand how the world works

Individuals whose energy signatures are rich in Fifth Ray energy become the chemists, biologists and physicists of the world. Souls with Fifth Ray energy are born with the desire to unlock the secrets of the material world. Whereas Third Ray souls are applied scientists and the creators of technology, Fifth Ray types live more in the realm of pure science and theory.

One example of a Fifth Ray reincarnation match involves the case of Benjamin Rush | Kary Mullis, which is featured in *Return of the Revolutionaries* and the expanded version of *Born Again.* Benjamin Rush was a leading chemist and phy-sician during the time of the American Revolution and Kary Mullis won the Nobel Prize in 1993 for inventing Polymerase Chain Reaction (PCR), which underlies the process of DNA fingerprinting. Kary and his wife, Nancy, agreed to be featured as reincarnation cases in *Revolutionaries.*

Ahtun Re has suggested that Albert Einstein and Nicolaus Copernicus were Fifth Ray types. It is proposed that Copernicus has reincarnated and is doing work very similar to what he did in the past. He is again a world expert on planetary motion, and has in fact served as a leader of the NASA Mars Rover project. Ahtun Re has affirmed that Copernicus has reincarnated as Ste-ven W. Squyres, a professor of astronomy at Cornell University. Like Copernicus, Squyres is interested in large bodies, such as planets and moons of our solar system. He was a student of Carl Sagan. Sagan, in a prior incarnation, as revealed in *Born Again* and *Return of the Revolutionaries,* was David Rittenhouse, American's first astronomer.

The reincarnation cases of both Copernicus | Squyres and Rittenhouse | Sagan show a marked similarity in their career paths, due in part to the expression of Fifth Ray energy in their incarnations.

It must be noted, however, that a particular profession may contain people of different ray energies. For example, medical doctors may be Fifth Ray types if they are research-oriented, Third Ray types if they are medical inventors, Second Ray types if they are drawn to societal and ethical issues involving medicine, or First Ray types if their propensity is to be chief of the medical staff or the director of a hospital.

Sixth Ray: the energy of devotion, which produces a desire to serve a religion, a cause or other people
Individuals with a great deal of Sixth Ray energy become the priests, rabbis and mullahs of the world. On an everyday level, the Sixth Ray energy of devotion can be seen as the ray of motherhood and maternal instinct. Mothers and women in general have a tendency to devote themselves to their children and families, to the ones they love. Mother Teresa is a classic example of the Sixth Ray type, as she not only served the Christian Church, but she was also devoted to ministering to the sick. Other historical examples of Sixth Ray types include St. Thomas, St. Augustine, St. Thomas Aquinas, St. John of the Cross and Pope John Paul II. Moses can be seen as a Sixth Ray type, though he also demonstrated First Ray qualities as a leader of the Hebrew people.

Ahtun Re has indicated that Martin Luther King, the Christian minister who led America out of segregation through nonviolent protest, was a Sixth Ray type. King used the Christian Church and religion as his chariot to emancipate African Americans from the residuals of slavery.

An example of an enlightened Sixth Ray soul is Jesus, who was called rabbi by his disciples, but who eventually transcended religious divisions. Interestingly, in a subsequent chapter, it will be proposed that Jesus himself has had prior incarnations.

Seventh Ray: the energy of organization, which produces a desire to create working systems

Individuals rich in Seventh Ray energy love to create systems and organizations that produce dynamic results. Seventh Ray types like to organize disparate parts into an efficient working whole. Seventh Ray souls may gravitate to organizations where there is an opportunity to create and implement working systems, such as in government or corporations. Political scientists who like to create constitutions that will help a society function effectively can be seen as Seventh Ray types. Whereas First Ray types may want to become leaders of organizations, Seventh Ray types are the creators of organizations and systems.

To utilize a musical analogy, whereas a Fourth Ray type may become a soloist who creates beautiful music on a particular instrument, Seventh Ray types prefer to become conductors who orchestrate many instruments to create a combined and complex sound. TV or movie producers who bring together writers, actors, musicians, cameramen and others can be seen as Seventh Ray types. Seventh Ray souls perceive that a group can attain a greater result than an individual. Examples of Seventh Ray types from the American Revolution will be provided in a later section.

The model of the Seven Rays is useful in understanding personality, which tends to be consistent from one lifetime to another. Which ray or rays do you identify with? By and large, the rays that you identify with and express are the rays that will characterize you from one incarnation to another. As noted, in expressing the rays, we can see ourselves as fountains that emit different combinations of colors of light.

Since we all have our own specific energy spectrum which is different than that of others, each of us will have a different path of evolution. The developmental path of one who expresses primarily First Ray energy will differ from that of an individual who tends to express Fourth Ray energy. The First Ray will pursue lifetimes in which leadership and the energy of will can be expressed, whereas the Fourth Ray type will develop artistic skills through a variety of incarnations. The diversity and richness of life comes from the varied contributions that the seven different ray types make to our world.

The Seven Rays is one model of personality that is useful in understanding the monad and the soul. The monad serves as a prism that separates the white light of God into a unique spectrum. The monad transmits this energy to the soul. The soul, in turn, creates a hologram that is focused into the physical body, a hologram that contains the energy spectrum of the monad and soul, as well as the various talents and abilities that the soul has accumulated through its incarnations.

I would now like to introduce the concept of dipole pairs, which pertain to the creation of monads and souls. The model of the Seven Rays will also be employed in our discussion of dipoles.

4

Soul Mates, Dipoles and the Story of Cain and Abel

As described in Kevin Ryerson's book, *Spirit Communication,* and affirmed by Ahtun Re, God created us not individually but in complementary pairs. These pairs were created with similar qualities, and if the model of the Seven Rays is used, these complementary pairs would be of the same ray. Still, they have contrasting characteristics within their common ray. On the physical plane, these pairs are often found on opposite sides of an issue and contrasting characteristics can lead to conflict.

In his book, Kevin Ryerson terms these pairs "soul mates," as they were created together to complement one another. For most people, the term "soul mate" implies a relationship in which two people are simpatico, where a great deal of resonance is felt and the relationship is characterized by harmony. Harmony, however, often does *not* characterize the relationship between paired souls. I prefer to refer to these original pairs, souls created at the same time by God, as "dipoles," as this term makes it clear that the pairs are of contrasting nature and that there is a potential aspect of conflict between them.

One can think of dipoles as the positive and negative poles of a magnet or battery. This does not imply that one dipole is good and the other is bad: rather, that they have contrasting and complementary qualities. In addition to differences in personality, dipoles often have contrasting appearances. One dipole may be thin and lanky while the other is stout.

In this book, the term "soul mates" will refer to two individuals who are highly compatible, who have had many, many lifetimes together, and who find that their relationships are marked by ease. Due to this inherent compatibility and shared experience, soul mates, when they first meet in a particular incarnation, feel like they have known each other forever. This experience is quite common and indeed, many find themselves believing in reincarnation, whatever their previous stance may have been, as it is the only way that such an innate attraction and sense of recognition can be explained.

Soul mates can return in different role relationships from one incarnation to another. They can come back as our parents, spouses, children, friends or business associates. Soul mates can also be of divergent ray types: they were not created as pairs, but they find that they are very much at ease with one another. Dipoles, by contrast, are souls that were created as pairs, souls of the same ray type but whose relationship can be marked by conflict.

Let us review a few dipole pairs, as identified by Ahtun Re and categorized by ray type. For those who are experts on the Seven Rays, I know that there are very complex systems which describe the ray structure of an individual. The examples provided below are used to demonstrate ray energies in a simple way for dipole pairs. We in truth are a combination of the rays.

First Ray Dipoles: A First Ray dipole pair identified in *Spirit Communication* involves Moshe Dyan and Anwar Sadat, both leaders of the Middle East but on opposite sides of the conflict there. Dyan was an Israeli leader while Sadat was an Egyptian statesman. Ahtun Re has explained that one reason that God created us in dipole pairs is so that no one soul becomes dominant over others, as a dominating soul's dipole, acting as an individual or leading a group, would produce a counteracting effect. This is particularly important for First Ray types, who have a predisposition to seek power.

This is why First Ray dipole pairs are often found on opposite sides of a conflict. By creating dipoles, God engineered balance in the course of human events, though it was not God's intent that dipoles fight each other. While the potential for conflict may be inherent in First Ray dipoles, the expression or lack or expression of conflict reflects the maturity and development of the respective souls.

A dipole pair from the American Revolution involves George Washington and Benedict Arnold. Washington and Arnold were both American Patriot military heroes of the early phase of the Revolutionary War, but they eventually found themselves on opposite sides when Arnold defected to the British Army. To the Patriots, Arnold was the ultimate traitor, whereas to Great Britain, he was a Loyalist and ally.

Ahtun Re has indicated that George Washington reincarnated as the Confederate soldier and West Virginia senator, John E. Kenna, then again as WWII General George Marshall, and more recently as US General Tommie Franks. Benedict Arnold has also reincarnated in contemporary times. He served as a decorated officer in the US Army in Vietnam, as did Franks.

The dipole pair of George Washington | Benedict Arnold makes us reflect on the observation that one man's hero can be another man's traitor. To add to the mix, opponents in one war can reincarnate to fight together on the same side in another, as demonstrated in the Washington and Arnold cases.

Jeff Keene's reincarnation case is featured in *Born Again* and *Return of the Revolutionaries*, in which Jeff unexpectedly discovered his past lifetime as John B. Gordon, a Confederate General in the American Civil War. In his book, *Someone Else's Yesterday,* Keene points out that as John B. Gordon of the Southern state of Georgia, he fought on the Confederate side, while in his current incarnation, he lives in Connecticut, a Northern state.

Jeff observes that in contemporary times, he has ancestors who fought for the North in the US Civil War, ancestors who may have actually fought against him when he was John B. Gordon! From the perspective of reincarnation, the world would be a much better place if we could work out differences peaceably and keep First Ray energy in check, for one way or another, we end up fighting ourselves.

Another dipole pair which involves First Ray energy involves the boxers Muhammad Ali and Joe Frazier. Ali can be described as thin, lanky, quick and bombastic, while Frazier has the characteristics of being stocky, powerful and more introverted. Their differences made their boxing matches some of the most dramatic in history.

So we see in these examples of how dipoles – who were created together as pairs and who demonstrate similar ray qualities – can end up having contrasting allegiances and may even end up fighting one another. Though Ahtun Re states that Cain and Abel of the Old Testament were actual historic individuals, the archetype of these two brothers, whose contrasting natures led to conflict, jealousy and murder, can be seen to represent dipoles. The observation of dipole pairs fighting each other in contemporary times can be as sad as it was in biblical times.

Second Ray Dipoles: Ahtun Re has indicated that Mahatma Gandhi and Jawaharlal Nehru, who were both scholars, were dipoles that demonstrated Second Ray energy. William Shakespeare and Christopher Marlowe have also been identified as dipoles of the Second Ray.

Third Ray Dipoles: Ahtun Re has indicated that Thomas Edison and Henry Ford were dipoles in the Third Ray category. Edison was a pioneering inventor of electrical devices while Ford changed the world by bringing the assembly line into practical use.

Fourth Ray Dipoles: Ahtun Re has indicated that Laurel & Hardy were Fourth Ray types and that they were dipoles. Note how Laurel & Hardy do represent opposites. Ollie was heavy and presented himself as worldly and all-knowing, while Stan was thin and portrayed himself as an innocent. In their routines, there is often an element of conflict between them, including slapstick violence.

The end result of their friction is the ignition of laughter, and Stan and Ollie eventually arrive at a harmonious, happy ending. Laurel & Hardy represent dipoles that have used their differences to humorous advantage. As revealed in *Born Again,* Stan and Ollie have reincarnated as Josh and Danny Bacher, who are motivated by the same desire as were Stan and Ollie, to give the world a few good laughs.

Of interest, in their movie *Flying Deuces,* Stan and Ollie discuss reincarnation. Ollie asks Stan what he would like to reincarnate as. Stan says that he would like to return as himself. Ollie, on the other hand, wants to return as a horse. At the end of the movie, after trying to fly an airplane in a haphazard way, they crash. On the ground, we see that Stan has survived, while a winged and semi-transparent Ollie floats up to heaven. Years later, Stan is walking by himself down a country road when he hears Ollie's voice. After surveying his surroundings, he is surprised to find Ollie's voice emanating from a horse who is wearing Ollie's derby hat as well as his trademark moustache.

As will be discussed, many eons ago, human souls did project themselves into animal forms and perhaps Ollie did, in bygone times, have four hoofs. In contemporary times though, Stan has returned as Josh and Ollie as his brother Danny. Animal costumes have replaced animal forms.

Another artistic dipole set involves the musicians John Lennon and Paul McCartney, whose contrasting natures and complementary talents synergized to create one of the greatest songwriting teams in history.

Fifth Ray Dipoles: A scientist dipole pair involves Robert Koch and Louis Pasteur, both of whom were pioneers of microbiology. As affirmed by Ahtun Re, Koch and Pasteur have reincarnated as biologists involved in mapping the human genome. Robert Koch has reincarnated as J. Craig Venter, founder of Celera Genomics, which conducted a program to map the human genome for commercial purposes. Louis Pasteur has reincarnated as Francis Collins, who has served as the director of the National Human Genome Research Institute. Though considered rivals, as were Koch and Pasteur, Venter and Collins jointly announced the successful mapping of the human genome in the year 2000.

Recall that Kary Mullis, who received the Nobel Prize for discovering Polymerase Chain Reaction (PCR), which underlies

DNA fingerprinting and contributed to DNA mapping, agreed to be featured as the reincarnation of Benjamin Rush in *Return of the Revolutionaries*. Dr. Mullis is also featured in the expanded version of *Born Again*. Kary Mullis is thus a colleague of Venter and Collins, one who believes in reincarnation.

Another dipole pair that demonstrates Fifth Ray qualities involves Charles Darwin and Jean-Baptiste Lamarck. Darwin advocated a theory of evolution that focused on the survival of the fittest. To him, members of a species with adaptive genetic attributes survived while those without those traits died. The surviving members of the species then propagated the adaptive traits through reproduction. As an example, giraffes with the longest necks were able to reach food in trees and survive, while giraffes with shorter necks died off. Giraffes with tall necks reproduced, creating more long-necked giraffes. Lamarck, on the other hand, proposed that individual members of a species could acquire adaptive traits within a lifetime. In the giraffe example, through biochemical changes, a giraffe could theoretically make its neck longer. Science remembers Darwin as the winner of this evolutionary debate.

Lamarck, interestingly, has reincarnated in the person of Bruce Lipton, PhD, a biochemist and former professor at Stanford University in California. In his book, *The Biology of Belief*, Dr. Lipton makes the case that Lamarck was right and he produces examples where organisms, including animals, have been able to generate adaptive characteristics through biochemical changes stimulated by environmental factors.

In reading *The Biology of Belief*, it is clear that Lipton is a fan of Lamarck and one gets the distinct impression that Lipton is vindicating Lamarck. As such, I consider the Lamarck | Lipton case to be an affinity case, in which Bruce Lipton was attracted to his own past-life persona, Lamarck. The Dorothy Dandridge | Halle Berry and the Laurel & Hardy | Bacher Boys cases, featured in *Born Again*, also represent affinity cases.

Sixth Ray Dipoles: Ahtun Re has indicated that St. Francis of Assisi and St. Clare of Assisi were dipole pairs, as were St. John of the Cross and St. Teresa of Avila. In contemporary times, Ahtun Re has confirmed that Saint Teresa has reincarnated as Susan Trout, the founder of the Institute for the Advancement of Service in Alexandria, Virginia. St. John of the Cross has also reincarnated and once again, he has served as St. Teresa's, that is, Susan's, mentor. Let us allow Susan to reflect on her past incarnation as St. Teresa in her own words, as her narrative beautifully illustrates how passions and aptitudes are re-expressed from one incarnation to another.

To complete our soul development in a single lifetime seems impossible to me. Each incarnation offers an opportunity to evolve different slices of our "soul-pie" until wholeness is attained. I believe that my present incarnation expresses this premise; I consider the awareness of any previous incarnations, such as that of Teresa of Avila, simply exists to help guide me to my True Home.

Forty years ago, I was told by a seer that I was a reincarnation of Teresa of Avila. This meant nothing to me at the time as I was raised in a fundamentalist Christian church and told that only men saints mentioned in the Bible were true saints. Knowledge about a Teresa incarnation came at a time in my life when I was in deep despair. Being told that I had once been a saint did not match my desperate state or my spiritual awareness. Nevertheless, I viewed the information as a message of hope. Subsequently, I have been told of my Teresa incarnation by other spiritual teachers, intuitives, gurus and Light Workers. I finally decided there was a reason I needed to learn about Teresa's life, which occurred some 500 years ago (1515–1582).

Much has been written about Teresa's life in Spain as a vigorous reformer of the Carmelite Order and a disciplined explorer of mystical experience. She had a gift for administration and a passion for direct conversation with God. She was considered willful, quirky, vain and visionary. She had a "mind of her own" and a fierce determination to go against Vatican control and establish convents to perpetuate her reform. Whenever I connect to Teresa, I sense the depth of her inner struggles and her profound desire to transcend her personality "quirks" and join God. I sense the truth that exists beneath her writings and beyond what others write about her. Her life was too much of a struggle for her to believe she was special in any way.

The following aspects of Teresa's nature seem to be part of my own. Some of what Teresa left undone in her spiritual life 500 years ago is what I seem to be determined to do in my own life. I brought some of her gifts and challenges forward into this life.

Spiritual Life: Like Teresa, devotion to God has been the primary focus of my life; all I have ever wanted to be was a willing instrument of God's Love in service to humanity. In my youth, I withdrew from organized Christianity because I felt it kept me "in kindergarten." Eventually, I found my spiritual home in Eastern Traditions and in metaphysics/Ancient Wisdom. I am broad-minded and effortlessly understand universal spiritual experiences and psychological and soul development. I recognize the validity of someone's psychological and/or spiritual experience even if I can't recall ever having that experience myself (in this life). Even as a youth, people described me as a very "deep" person, perhaps a Teresa quality.

Writing: I have written two books that I feel are sequels to Teresa's *The Interior Castle*. I have had a lifelong interest in understanding soul development, leadership and service. I felt inspired to write about soul development and service, taking Teresa's castle metaphor of the soul to its next step. I wrote *Born to Serve: The Evolution of the Soul Through Service* in 1997 and *The Awakened Leader: Leadership as a Classroom of the Soul* in 2005.

Physical Likeness: Much is written about Teresa's attractiveness and the fact she did not age until a year before her death at age 68. No photograph exists of Teresa; a painting was done when she was in her early 60s, about which Teresa commented that because the painter made her look ugly, she would accept it as an opportunity to develop humility. Authors write often about the beauty of her skin, eyes, hands and feet. As long as I can remember, people have "made a big deal" about the beauty of my skin, eyes, hands and feet.

Determination: I join Teresa in being described by others as having an extremely strong and developed will and a determination that defies description. Like Teresa, I am determined to follow my vision and bring it into reality by integrating psychological principles, spiritual ideals and right action.

Nun-Likeness: Throughout my life, colleagues, students and friends have told me I look like a nun, act like a nun, and lead like a Mother Superior. Catholic nuns I know claim I lead organizations like a true convent, evidenced by stressing coherence of universal psychological and spiritual principles with action in the world and by holding high standards for myself and for others. Unlike Teresa, I am not an extravert nor do I have a buoyant personality. I tend to "hide" my Light. . . this is in contrast to Teresa, who was expressive in a dramatic way. I feel this shift is an attempt to balance outer and inner energies. Also, I have had to learn how to balance care of self with care of others; Teresa sacrificed her own needs for others and I have the same strong tendency. This imbalance adversely impacted Teresa's physical and emotional health as it has mine.

Reformer: Just as Teresa was a founder and leader of the reformed Carmelite order, I have been a reformer, leader and founder of departments, personal growth and healing methodologies, professions and organizations. Like Teresa, I am intensely driven to bring what is off-course back into integrity with its true course. Teresa, however, at times lowered her standards with those she felt would financially support her convents.

In this life, I have refused to lower my ethical standards for any reason. This has not made me popular at times for difficult decisions I have had to make, especially in the workplace.

Leader, Organizer, and Administrator: Like Teresa, I am described as incredibly organized and having a sixth sense for how to found, direct, and administer an organization. My parents claim I was "born organized" and my colleagues say I run a "well-oiled machine." Nothing misses my eyes and their appreciation for the blending of detail with beauty.

Women: As a helping professional and as a trainer of professionals in both university and non-profit settings, I have been surrounded by women. I am often their counselor, guide and teacher. Teresa felt she neglected the care and well-being of many of her nuns as funds were not always available and she could not regularly visit and oversee the well-being of the nunneries she founded. This lifetime, I have felt I had karma with many women (former nuns?) and have wanted to correct these relationships. At times, I have confronted a person on an issue in this life because I had neglected to do so in Teresa's life. I have never wanted to be part of a school of thought with multiple centers because I understood that it was nearly impossible to ethically oversee their well-being.

Men: Much has been written about Teresa's attraction to men and they to her; she was believed to manipulate men often and they her, so that she would obtain the needed funds and housing for her convents. In this life, I have attempted to develop healthy working relationships with men and learn to understand and respect them. I am steadfast in not tolerating unethical behavior on the part of men. Except for a brief marriage, I, like Teresa, have not chosen a life path of marriage and children.

John of the Cross: Juan de la Cruz, a Carmelite monk, was twenty-five and about to become a hermit in the Primitive Rule of his order when he met fifty-year-old Teresa. Teresa persuaded him to head her monastic foundations and be her strong right arm in managing the convents. He eventually became her spiritual director. They were known to love and respect one another dearly, despite their differing natures. Marcelle Auclair, one of Teresa's most insightful biographers, compared the two: "For her, to love was to act. For him, to love was to immerse oneself completely in contemplation." After her death at age 68, Juan de la Cruz assumed leadership of the convents to ensure her work would continue.

In 1982, I met a well-known and respected spiritual teacher whom I immediately recognized as John of the Cross. We have since spoken of the Teresa-Juan incarnation. In this life, I seek his counsel much as I did when he was Teresa's spiritual director 500 years ago. I respect his wish not to be named.

Conclusion: The Teresa incarnation has been a way-shower for my spiritual development in this life. It has helped me stay on purpose with my soul development and service and not get lost in the material world. I can choose to evolve and be aware of patterns that disrupted my spiritual growth in a previous life and seek to dissolve them in this one. Remembering Teresa is remembering my True Identity.

– Susan Trout, November 19, 2006

In Susan's narrative, it is noted that St. Teresa and John of the Cross were of contrasting natures. Teresa expressed divinity in action while John sought divinity in contemplation. Conflict, though, is not a requirement of dipole pairs, especially if they are enlightened. For example, Ahtun Re has revealed that Mary, the Virgin Mother, and Jesus were dipole pairs, created at the same time by God to complement one another.

Seventh Ray Dipoles: Seventh Ray energy, we recall, involves organization and the creation of functioning systems. One Seventh Ray dipole pair offered by Ahtun Re involves James Madison, who was heavily involved in drafting the Federal Constitution of the United States, and Alexander Hamilton, who was an architect of the financial system of the new country.

Ahtun Re has indicated that another Seventh Ray dipole pair from the American Revolution involves John Adams and Thomas Jefferson. Adams was very proud of writing the first constitution in the colonies, the Massachusetts Constitution, which served as a model for the Federal Constitution. Adams called his constitution, "my system," whose chief feature was the separation and balancing of power between the executive, legislative and judicial branches of government.

Adams, like Washington, was a proponent of a strong central or federal government. Jefferson was the principal author of the Declaration of Independence, though Adams served on the Declaration committee. In contrast to Adams, Jefferson was vested in a system with states having equal or more power relative to the central, federal government. In addition to these political differences, note that Jefferson was tall and lanky, while Adams was shorter but very muscular.

Even geographically, Adams and Jefferson contrasted, with Adams residing in the North, in Massachusetts, and Jefferson in the South, in Virginia. Their mutual friend, Benjamin Rush, alluded to the contrasting nature of this Seventh Ray dipole pair, writing that Adams and Jefferson were the "North and South Pole of the American Revolution." In a final, interesting twist of fate that seems to reflect their dipole nature, Adams and Jefferson both died on July 4, 1826, on the 50th anniversary of the Declaration of Independence.

5

Split Incarnation or Parallel Lives

At this point, I would like to make a distinction between dipoles and "splits." In contrast to dipole pairs, where two different but complementary souls were created at the same time, split incarnation refers to the phenomenon where one soul animates two or more human bodies at the same time. In split incarnation, the "splits" have similar facial features, personality traits and aptitudes, as they derive from the same soul. Dipoles, on the other hand, have different facial features and they typically have contrasting body types.

The reincarnation cases involving Penney Peirce, presented in *Born Again* and *Return of the Revolutionaries,* provide compelling evidence of the phenomenon of split incarnation. Many reincarnation cases researched by Ian Stevenson, MD at the University of Virginia, also demonstrate split incarnation. Dr. Stevenson referred to these as cases with "anomalous dates," as lifetimes were observed to overlap. Another term for split incarnation is parallel lives. Stevenson split incarnation cases are compiled and can be reviewed at:

www.ReincarnationResearch.com

The Split Incarnation Case of Sir George Hubert Wilkins|Edgar Mitchell, PhD

Another fascinating split reincarnation case involves Edgar Mitchell, an Apollo astronaut and founder of the Institute of Noetic Sciences (IONS). I encountered this case in 2011, as I was traveling by train from Liverpool to London. On this journey, I was reading *The Power of Premonitions*, by Larry Dossey, MD, which features a chapter entitled *Across Space and Time: Two Explorers Test the Limits of Premonitions.*[1] In this chapter, Dr. Dossey describes how the Australian native, Sir George Hubert Wilkins, was a real-life superhero who was the first to fly an aircraft across the northern polar ice cap in 1928, and who was also a war hero and scientist.

Wilkins grew up with the aborigine people and he noticed that they seemed capable "of knowing of some event which was taking place beyond their range of sight and hearing."[2] When Wilkins went on a rescue operation to Alaska, he decided to see if he could send telepathic messages to a collaborator in New York named Harold Sherman, who was a psychic and writer.

Over a period of 6 months, Wilkins would write a log of events that transpired in Alaska and attempt to send telepathic messages to Sherman regarding these events. Sherman would receive impressions, theoretically from Wilkins, and write them down. When an independent evaluator correlated Wilkins' written log to Sherman's written impressions, a 60% correspondence was found, where many very specific items matched.

Dr. Dossey then explains that Edgar Mitchell, who is a retired Navy aircraft carrier fighter pilot and US astronaut, replicated the telepathy experiments of Wilkins and Sherman. When Edgar Mitchell served as the lunar module pilot for Apollo 14, he did an experiment in which he tried to send telepathic messages from outer space to human receivers on Earth. The experiment was successful.

Dr. Dossey then makes the comment that the experiment done by Wilkins from the Arctic to New York, spanning 3400 miles, was replicated by Edgar Mitchell, who sent telepathic messages across 200,000 miles from outer space.

It is evident from reincarnation research that individuals replicate talents, patterns and behaviors from lifetime to lifetime. Such similarities between these two men are obvious. Wilkins was a pioneering pilot, war hero, scientist and experimenter in telepathy. Edgar Mitchell is a retired Navy pilot, Apollo astronaut, doctoral graduate from the Massachusetts Institute of Technology (MIT) in Aeronautics and Astronautics, telepathy experimenter and founder of the Institute of Noetic Sciences, which is dedicated to better understanding subjects such as consciousness, telepathy and psychokinesis.

As such, it was natural for me to wonder whether Edgar Mitchell is the reincarnation of Sir George Hubert Wilkins. Reincarnation research also demonstrates that individuals have the same physical appearance, the same facial features, from lifetime to lifetime. As I was traveling on the *Virgin* train from Liverpool to London, I used the Internet to see if Edgar Mitchell resembles Wilkins. I found that they do indeed have similar facial features.

In a subsequent session with Kevin Ryerson, Ahtun Re affirmed that Mitchell is the reincarnation of Wilkins. Of interest, Harold Sherman, who did the telepathy experiments with Wilkins, has also worked with Edgar Mitchell, demonstrating how a relationship can extend across two lifetimes.

The Wilkins | Mitchell case, if accepted, represents another example of split incarnation as Wilkins died in 1958, while Edgar Mitchell was born in 1930. As such, the lifetimes of Wilkins and Mitchell have overlapped by 28 years, which is similar to the overlap demonstrated in the split incarnation case involving Penney Pierce.

The Mechanism and Purpose of Split Incarnation

Ahtun Re has indicated that the ability of the soul to inhabit more than one human body at a time is a developed skill. Just as the novice juggler first learns to control one ball before throwing a second and third ball in the air, souls must develop before they are able to control or animate more than one physical body at a time.

Another analogy that can be used to visualize how split incarnation works is to think of a drummer in a band, who is beating the snare drum with one hand, a cymbal with the other hand, a bass drum with one foot and another percussive device with the other foot. The drummer's hands and feet are all functioning independently in performing sophisticated and complex maneuvers, yet it is the mind or nervous system of the drummer that is coordinating the movement of all the separate parts or extremities. In the same way, the soul can be seen as the mind of the drummer and the drummer's arms and legs can be seen as the soul's splits who have their own existences on the physical plane. Of course, before the drummer could play complex patterns, as a novice, he beat one drum at a time.

The analogy of the drummer is also useful in understanding that a soul can communicate through a medium while it also has an incarnation on the physical plane. A drummer can sing or communicate vocally while the drummer's arms and legs are still operating various components of a drum set. Similarly, Ahtun Re could theoretically be channeled through Kevin Ryerson while having an incarnation on the physical plane at the same time.

Another way to visualize split incarnation is to utilize our concept of the soul projecting holograms or three-dimensional images of itself. It was previously suggested that the soul projects a hologram into the developing physical body that serves as a template for bone and tissue. Just as orthopedic surgeons use bone stimulators that utilize electrical current to help stimulate the growth of bone, the soul's hologram serves to shape bone and tissue so that we have similar facial features from one incarnation to another.

In the phenomenon of splits, the soul projects more than one hologram at a time. As an example, the soul can project a hologram into a physical body in the United States while projecting another in India or China. The soul's splits all have the same facial architecture and same basic energies, the same energy spectrum or ray pattern, though racial and cultural differences will influence expression of the hologram.

In this context, I would like to bring up an issue that the reader may have wondered about as to why so many reincarnated historical figures are found, as least according to *Born Again* and *Return of the Revolutionaries,* reborn today in the United States. The reason is simply that my cultural background is the English-speaking world, so it is much easier for me to research reincarnation cases in this culture. It is easier for me to identify reincarnated individuals in the United States. For developed souls, splits are also likely to be incarnated in other cultures, but these splits have not been identified by me due to barriers of language and access to information.

Ahtun Re has indicated that currently, at the present state of human evolution, about three percent of souls on Earth are able to have split incarnations. If one assumes that each soul that is capable of having splits has two incarnations at a time, then six percent of the people on Earth represent splits. As such, there are many splits incarnate in the world today where a soul has two or perhaps three bodies that it inhabits at a time. Ahtun Re has stated that the maximum number of splits that a soul can have at the present stage of human evolution is about seven, though this is a very rare phenomenon.

There are several pairs of splits that we have currently identified. For example, I had the pleasure of meeting a split of mine in 2006 when I visited India. My split, like me, studied biology and graduated with honors at an established university. Like me, my split has shifted his life's work from biology to reincarnation research. We share similar facial features, body types and personality traits. While my focus is on objective evidence of reincarnation, the focus of my split is on past-life regression therapy. Ahtun Re has pointed out that my split and I demonstrate how a soul can implement a division of labor through parallel lives. I am chiefly concerned with objective evidence of reincarnation while my split works with the subjective realm.

Why would a soul choose to have splits? One reason is the possibility for karma to be worked out in a more efficient manner, as one split can deal with one set of karmic lessons to work through while another split deals with another set. At times, the usual gifts that a soul possesses, which in past lives have brought wealth or fame, may need to be blocked so that lessons involving humility or personal relationships can be learned. One split may have long-developed talents blocked so as to work instead on empathy and humility, while the other split is allowed to express innate talents to help humanity.

As mentioned above regarding my split in India, having splits can allow for a division of labor. Having splits in diverse geographical settings also allows for a more global approach to projects. As reincarnation research progresses, given the ability for people to communicate around the world through the Internet, more splits will recognize one another and will work together, hopefully for the betterment of humanity.

Having drawn the distinction between dipole pairs and splits, let us now return to models of personality to better understand the nature of the soul and energy spectrums.

6

Astrology, the Kabbalah, the Enneagram and Your Energy Spectrum

Having covered several other topics, including the creation of the universe, monads and souls, dipoles and split incarnation, I would like to return to the topic of one's energy spectrum or energy signature. The model of the Seven Rays was used to visualize and understand how we all have a stable set of energies that we bring with us from one incarnation to another. This energy signature predisposes us to specific talents, passions and behaviors. We will now review other models which can be used to understand our energy spectrums, the systems of astrology, the Kabbalah and the Enneagram.

Astrology and Reincarnation

I approached astrology many years ago with the skeptical attitude of a scientist who wanted to know why astrology had such a lock on the minds of people everywhere. Though astrology seemed implausible from a rational point of view, horoscope columns appear in almost every newspaper in the world. I wanted to know why. My search eventually even led me to write a book entitled *Astrology for Regular People,* in which I attempted to explain the complex world of astrology in simple, easy to understand ways. I even used cartoon characters to make the archetypes of astrology, the signs, planets and houses of astrology, easy to comprehend.

Two main branches of astrology that I became interested in and wrote about are natal horoscope astrology and the astrological transits. Natal horoscope astrology deals with explaining one's personality based on the location of the planets in the signs and houses of the zodiac. The zodiac is the array of the twelve constellations of astrology – Aries, Taurus, etc. through to Pisces – which encircle the Earth. These constellations are on the same plane as the sun and the planets of our solar system.

At the moment one is born, if you look at our Sun from the vantage point of the Earth, one of the constellations of the zodiac will be found behind or in the background of the Sun. This constellation, which the Sun is said to be sitting in, is defined as your Sun sign. For example, if at the moment of your birth, the Sun, from the vantage point of the Earth, is lined up with the constellation Virgo in the background, then your Sun sign or "sign" is Virgo.

Further, imagine that at the moment you are born, a snapshot is taken which identifies the position of all of the planets in our solar system in relation to the constellations of the zodiac. This snapshot creates what astrologers call your natal horoscope or chart. The placement of the various planets in the twelve signs, as well as the geometric interrelationships that bind them such as conjunctions, squares, trines or sextiles, are thought by astrologers to determine one's personality.

The other branch of astrology that I studied, the astrological transits, involves the real planets in space orbiting over time in our solar system and the geometric angles that these planets make to one's natal horoscope. The transits are the basis of most predictions made in astrology. For example, according to transit astrology, if orbiting Jupiter, which is the planet of bestowal, passes the position that Venus was in at the time of your birth, which is the location of Venus in your natal horoscope, there is a higher probability that a love relationship will manifest in your life at that time, as Venus is associated with love relationships. Transit astrology is fascinating, though there is the danger of becoming obsessed with observing one's transits, wondering what may occur during important transits.

It would be interesting to study transit astrology scientifically, as this branch of astrology deals with specific types of events and psychological states which are supposed to occur at defined periods of time. Academic assessment of the transits has been attempted at the California Institute of Integral Studies in San Francisco by Stanislav Grof, MD, who is considered a founder of Transpersonal Psychology, and Richard Tarnas, PhD, who authored the classic philosophy book, *The Passion of the Western Mind*. Dr. Tarnas has written a book on his study of the transits entitled *Cosmos and Psyche,* which focuses on how astrological transits may have influenced the consciousness of humanity over the ages.

Let me now return to natal horoscope astrology, the branch of astrology that deals with personality determination, in light of the reincarnation research that has been presented in this book, *Born Again* and in *Return of the Revolutionaries*. In analyzing reincarnation cases and astrological charts from one incarnation to another, it has been my observation that natal horoscope charts can change considerably from one lifetime to another, but that personality traits tend to stay consistent.

In my discussions with Kevin Ryerson, Kevin coined the term "core essence" to describe the features of personality that remain the same from one incarnation to another, which appears to be independent of astrology or other factors. Your core essence seems to stay the same from one incarnation to another, regardless of the natal horoscope. Your core essence is essentially the same thing as your energy spectrum or energy signature.

Let us review some cases to better understand this point. In the case of John B. Gordon | Jeffrey Keene, not only is facial architecture the same, but even writing structure has been demonstrated to be consistent through a formal linguistic analysis. This linguistic analysis is provided in *Born Again* and *Return of the Revolutionaries,* as well as Jeff's book, *Someone Else's Yesterday.* Natal horoscope astrology could never predict such a specific similarity in traits across incarnations. Indeed, due to differences in the horoscopes of Gordon and Keene, one would expect differences, not similarities.

Let us refer to the following cases presented in *Born Again.* Consider the reincarnation case of Anne Frank | Barbro Karlen, where Barbro Karlen became a childhood writing prodigy, like Anne Frank, and even wrote on similar themes. In the case of Paul Gauguin | Peter Teekamp, Peter unconsciously replicated sketches that Gauguin drew, though at a younger age. Alexandra Nechita began creating art like Picasso when she was four years old and was called a "Petite Picasso" by the age of eight. Josh and Danny Bacher began impersonating Laurel and Hardy as children, and related to each other as Laurel and Hardy did. They recreated the artistic development of the comedic duo in producing their own silent movie in this lifetime, in an age when no other comedians are creating silent movies.

Astrology cannot explain such consistency in personality. Astrology cannot account for passions and talents remaining consistent from one lifetime to another and indeed, since horoscopes change from lifetime to lifetime, natal horoscope astrology would predict differences in character and life paths.

In sum, though I cannot state that the natal horoscope has no effect on personality, I can conclude in reviewing reincarnation cases and natal horoscopes that astrology has, at most, a minimal effect on personality traits as compared to the influence of one's core essence or energy spectrum, which remains consistent from incarnation to incarnation.

Some astrologers use techniques utilizing the nodes of the moon to predict what will happen across incarnations. But just as natal horoscope astrology does not, in my observation, seem to have a major effect on personality in one's current lifetime, it is hard for me to imagine astrology having much bearing on a future lifetime either. Decisions regarding future incarnations are complex ones that are influenced by our karma and desires as well as the decisions made by other members of our soul group.

Decisions are made as a group concerning incarnations, as observed in the phenomenon of family members and friends re-incarnating together. In my analysis, your soul is really the one in charge of planning an incarnation, not the alignment of the moon or other heavenly bodies found on an astrological chart from a previous incarnation.

One question that remains is: why then do some people seem to have very positive experiences when they consult astrologers? I believe that one reason is that successful astrologers have intuitive or psychic gifts and that they use the natal horoscope or the transits as tools to psychically tune into their clients.

Mitchell Gibson, MD, a psychiatrist who has written a book on astrology, points out that when an astrologer considers a client's horoscope – when all the variables such as the signs, planets, houses and the various geometric relationships that can be analyzed in reading a chart are taken into account – the astrologer has an enormous number of variables that can be considered. As such, the chart can be interpreted in thousands of ways with differing results. How does the astrologer even decide what part of the chart to look at? Again, I believe that the successful astrologer uses intuitive or psychic gifts in giving an accurate or meaningful reading.

Of course, the scientific community has long dismissed natal horoscope astrology, which again begs the question: why is astrology still so popular in the minds of people all over the world? My conclusion, which I arrived at even before I became involved in reincarnation research, is that astrology provides a model of personality that is one of the most comprehensive to ever exist, one that resonates in the minds and hearts of a broad spectrum of people.

Even if astrology does not determine personality, the archetypes of astrology do help people conceptualize personality types. For example, if one is neat and compulsive, it is common to describe these traits as those typical of Virgo. An astrologer would then look for some important aspect in the chart that involves Virgo. It is important to note, though, that astrologers cannot give accurate readings "blind," using only the horoscope. The astrologer must establish a personal relationship with an individual before a horoscope can be read, supporting the premise that successful astrologers use normal perception, as well as intuitive gifts, in serving their clients.

The archetypes of astrology can be used to understand one's energy spectrum or core essence, which remains the same from one incarnation to another. Much as we utilized the Seven Rays as a model of personality to understand our energy spectrum, we can also use astrology in the same way. The key is that the natal horoscope does not determine one's personality; rather, the archetypes of astrology can simply be used to describe elements of personality.

Astrology as a Model of Personality

In my study of astrology, I found it useful to understand the planets as archetypes or core symbols which underlie other concepts found in astrology. For example, the planet Mars embodies the same energies as the sign Aries. I will now review the archetypes of astrology drawn from my book, *Astrology for Regular People.* As you read, see which planets and signs you relate to.

- The Sun in astrology reflects your ego, your sense of self. The Sun is considered to be the primary archetype, or the ruler, of the sign Leo. Leo is symbolized by the lion, the king of the jungle, and Leo types like to be the center of attention, the star of the show, the king of the court. In *Astrology for Regular People*, the Sun is represented by a politician who enjoys radiating his smile to constituents at public forums. The Sun could also be represented as an actor or actress on stage.

- The Moon represents our emotional and nurturing nature; it is the archetype of the mother. The Moon is represented by a round-faced mom who drives a Moonmobile, a mini-van, which she uses to cart her little loved ones to school and to the grocery store to buy food to feed the ones she loves. The Moon is the archetype of the sign Cancer.

- Mercury represents our ability to intelligently analyze the concrete world; it represents the linear, reductive thought characteristic of the left side of the brain. Mercury is skilled at mathematics and language. Mercury is personified as a university professor. It is akin to Fifth Ray energy. In astrology, Mercury rules the sign Gemini, which is associated with rational thought, language and communication. Mercury also rules the sign Virgo, which embodies intelligent service. Virgo, always thinking, strives for perfection.

- Venus represents our ability to attract others; it is associated with beauty and beautiful things like art. In this way, Venus is consistent with Fourth Ray energy. Venus can be personified as a fashion model who is in love with love and objects of beauty. Venus rules the sign Taurus, the bull, which is associated with earthiness, stubbornness and a desire to possess things of beauty. Venus also rules the sign Libra, which is concerned with relationships and art. The symbol of Libra is a set of scales. In relationships, there is always give and take, and in art, there is a balancing of contrasting features, colors, shades, melodies, plots and subplots.

- Mars is the warrior in each of us, the part that has courage, strength, determination, willpower, daring and fight. In these ways, Mars embodies First Ray energy. Mars, in *Astrology for Regular People,* is personified as a football star who in his youth gets into a brawl and accidentally kills a man. Mars, in maturity, uses his courage to work with and confront gang members to prevent violence. Mars rules Aries, the ram, who charges at anyone or anything that gets in its way.

- Jupiter is the archetype of expansion, growth and bestowal. Monetary expansion can occur through business ventures. Intellectual expansion can occur through philosophical inquiry and physical expansion can occur through overeating, as Jupiter is a sensual sort. Jupiter tends to be happy and buoyant. Jupiter's philosophical side embodies Second Ray energy and indeed,

Jupiter, like Second Ray types, is charismatic. Jupiter rules the sign Sagittarius, symbolized by the philosophical, exploring and adventurous centaur who holds a bow, pointing his arrow at the mysteries of existence.

* Saturn represents discipline, the overcoming of obstacles and hardship which results in the development of endurance. As an archetype, Saturn can be personified by an athletics coach or a military drill sergeant. Saturn can also be seen as a sports referee, wearing a black and white striped shirt that represents rules and regulations. In this light, Saturn is associated with karma. Saturn rules the sign of Capricorn, represented by the goat, an animal that is stable, careful, disciplined, pragmatic and tough. Capricorn seeks social recognition through hard-earned gains.

* Uranus is the rebel, the revolutionary, the one who gets unexpected insights through intuitive, right-brain thinking. Uranus is associated with sudden, unexpected changes. Uranus rules the sign Aquarius, which is the sign of new and revolutionary ideas. The symbol of Aquarius is the water bearer, an individual kneeling down and pouring water out of an urn. The water symbolizes new ideas, which emerge out of Aquarius.

* Neptune represents universal love, merger and psychic awareness. If the ego is the part of us that makes us separate and distinct from others, Neptune dissolves the ego so that we become aware of our interconnectedness with all things. In *Astrology for Regular People,* Neptune is personified by a guitarist who melds or merges with music, at times even losing his sense of self. Neptune rules the sign Pisces, the fish, which is also a symbol of Jesus. Indeed, when Jesus states, "I and the Father are One," and "I am the true vine," he is embodying the archetypes of Neptune and Pisces in which an individual becomes one with a greater whole.

* Pluto is the planet of deep transformation, which forces one to reinvent or recreate oneself, which requires great determination

and will. Pluto has been associated with underworld figures due to the tendency to exert will regardless of consequences. On the positive side, Pluto is the planet of evolution and reformation. If Neptune represents the enlightened Jesus who could say, "I and the Father are One," Pluto is the energy that brought Jesus to the desert, where he spent 40 days and emerged transformed. Pluto rules the sign Scorpio. Individuals who demonstrate energies of Pluto and Scorpio use will to transform and reinvent.

So, in a relatively short space, we have defined the archetypes of astrology, of the planets and the signs. Rather than believing that the positions of the planets and stars determine our personality, let us view astrology as a model of personality.

As an exercise, why not review the archetypes of astrology as well as the Seven Rays and determine which archetypes you relate to the most. Write down these archetypes, for they make up your energy spectrum, your core essence, a set of energies that you were endowed with when your monad and soul were created just after the Big Bang. These are the energies and qualities that will typify you from one incarnation to another.

The Kabbalah, the Enneagram and Other Systems

There are other models of personality and other cosmologies that can be utilized in understanding human character. The Kabbalah is a fascinating Jewish mystical text that describes ten Sephirot which are enumerations, emanations or attributes of God. These, in turn, can be seen as attributes of humans, as the human soul is considered to be part of the Creator.

Reflect on the following quotation from Rabbi Yehuda Ashlag, a 19th century commentator on the Kabbalah: "The human soul is a part of the Creator [that is, Divine Light]. Therefore, there is no difference between Him and the soul. The difference is that He is the 'whole' and the soul is a 'part.' This resembles a stone carved from a rock. There is no difference between the stone and the rock except that the rock is a 'whole' and the stone is a 'part.'"

In this light, the emanations of God, the Sephirot, can be seen as akin to the model of the Seven Rays, where the white light of God is separated into separate energies. Some have drawn correspondences between the Sephirot and the planets of astrology. For example, the Sephirah or emanation of God named "Gevurah" is characterized by strength, determination, judgment and power. As such, Gevurah has been compared to the energy of Mars. The Sephirah of "Netzach" has been compared to the energy of Venus, symbolizing creativity and art.

The Enneagram is a model of personality that has enjoyed some popularity in recent years, which defines nine character types. Each type is given a number, from one through nine. Interestingly, each type is given a specific symbol reminiscent of astrological glyphs. A brief description of the Enneagram personality types is provided below:

Ones: reformers, who feel a need to make the world a better place

Twos: caretakers, who need to express love to others by giving and who desire to be loved in return

Threes: achievers, who need to succeed in tasks to feel appreciated

Fours: romantics, who demonstrate individualism through a creative process such as art

Fives: thinkers, who want to understand the world through facts

Sixes: loyalists, who desire stability

Sevens: adventurers, who live in the moment

Eights: leaders, who want to exert control through power

Nines: peacemakers, who are empathic and prefer calm over conflict

In all of the systems presented – the Seven Rays, the planets and signs of astrology, the Sephirot of the Kabbalah and the character types of the Enneagram – attempts are made to explain the diverse manifestations of humanity. Use whichever system appeals to you, or mix and match, to identify the archetypes that are strongest in your nature.

Reincarnation research reveals that our personality, character, passions and talents remain consistent from one incarnation to another, indicating that we do have an energy spectrum or core essence that manifests in similar ways from one incarnation to another. All models of personality attempt to describe this energy spectrum, though different symbols, terms or archetypes are used.

One value of these models is that in each of them, an archetype or energy can be seen as having positive or negative manifestations. The energy of will depicted as the First Ray, Mars, Aries or Gevurah, can be used to harm others, or the same energy of will can be used to help others.

Indeed, a key purpose of reincarnation is for all of us to learn to use the energy of will, to learn to use power, in such a way that we help our fellow human beings and other creatures rather than applying that energy to harm or control others. It is useful to understand your energy signature, using terms that appeal to you, so that you can apply your energies consciously and constructively.

7

Expressing Your Core Essence

Though one's core essence or spectrum of energies remains consistent from lifetime to lifetime, the expression of talents and the level of accomplishment can vary, based on genetic, biological, social and psychological factors.

Genetics and Biology

We have seen how facial features and in particular, bone structure, appear to remain consistent from one lifetime to another, which suggests that the soul produces an energy template that the body molds to. We have also entertained the thought that the soul projects a hologram into the developing body. In Theosophical literature, the term "etheric body" is used to describe an energy body that underlies the physical body. Though there does appear to be a template that influences bone structure and appearance, biological and genetic factors do play a role as well.

As an example, in *Born Again* and *Return of the Revolutionaries,* TV personality Oprah Winfrey is identified as the reincarnation of an orator of the American Revolution, James Wilson, who also taught English literature at the College of Philadelphia. Wilson's gift for oratory is expressed in Oprah, who won awards as a speaker in childhood and as an adolescent. Wilson's love of literature is reflected in Oprah's Book Club.

In terms of physical appearance, though Oprah and Wilson have near-identical bone structure, Oprah was born an African-American, and this change in race brings with it skin features characteristic of African-Americans. In the case of James Wilson | Oprah Winfrey, we observe how the energy template of the soul interacts with genetic factors in producing physical appearance.

People sometimes don't like the idea that facial features seem to remain consistent from lifetime to lifetime, particularly if they don't like their appearance in contemporary times. I always point out that facial architecture or bone structure can be perceived as beautiful or unattractive based on the overlay of factors unique to each lifetime such as complexion, condition of the teeth, height and body weight.

Above and beyond physical traits, the expression of intellectual capacity can be modified by genetic factors such as being born into a body in which the brain demonstrates dyslexia or other abnormalities. A soul may actually choose to be born into such a body based on lessons that need to be learned. For example, if a soul has demonstrated great intellectual prowess in past lifetimes and the individual has placed intellectual achievement above family and emotional relationships, the soul may chose to be born into a body where intellectual achievement is blocked so that the focus can be placed on emotional growth, as demonstrated by the development of traits such as empathy and learning to nurture others.

Social and Karmic Factors

Achievement may be moderated by social factors such as the socioeconomic status that one is born into. For example, an individual may be born into a situation where wealth and familial connections allow that person to pursue a political career and even become a historical figure. A good example involves the case of Daniel Morgan | George W. Bush, which is presented in *Born Again* and *Return of the Revolutionaries.*

Ahtun Re has indicated that the soul of Morgan purposefully incarnated into the Bush family in contemporary times for political advantage, as the soul wanted to pursue political office to complete a process started in the American Revolution. By incarnating as a son of former president George Herbert Walker Bush, the soul of Daniel Morgan, in the person of George W. Bush, was trained for a career in politics all throughout his upbringing.

On the other hand, if a soul plans to work on other issues such as personal relationships, then a different setting may be sought. As an example, Thomas Jefferson has reincarnated in contemporary times with very similar intellectual aptitudes as he had before. The contemporary Jefferson, who we will call Tom, has a PhD in education and he has had a career as an educator, which reflects Jefferson's founding of the University of Virginia.

Though he has had no formal training, Tom discovered that he has a natural ability to do architectural drawings, which represents a talent tapped from his Jefferson lifetime. Whereas Jefferson lost his wife at an early point in his life, Tom has enjoyed a long and happy marriage, though it is with a different soul as his current spouse. Whereas Jefferson ran for public office, Tom by contrast, in contemporary times, has lived a private life.

Tom, in this lifetime, has had an interesting learning experience that he has allowed me to share with you. In his youth, Tom volunteered to serve in the Peace Corps. Though he requested other destinations, he was assigned to Liberia, which is a country that Thomas Jefferson helped create to take in freed American slaves.

Tom served as a teacher on a plantation in Liberia that had electricity only two hours per day and water that was tapped from a well. Tom reflects that as much as is possible in modern times, this setting recreated plantation life at the time of the American Revolution. Thus, in contemporary times, Tom has served plantation workers as a teacher, whereas in colonial America, plantation slaves served him as Jefferson.

This is an example of how a soul, though demonstrating the same talents and aptitudes, can be famous in one incarnation and relatively unknown in another.

Psychological Factors

Talents can also be blocked by the soul because of past trauma or aversion, or simply to facilitate a different life path. A good example involves the case of Police Captain Robert Snow, who, during a past-life regression, remembered an incarnation as artist Carroll Beckwith. The case of Carroll Beckwith | Robert Snow is featured in *Born Again* and *Return of the Revolutionaries*. Captain Snow points out that in contemporary times, he has no artistic ability at all. When I asked Kevin Ryerson's guide about this, Ahtun Re indicated that Captain Snow has blocked the artistic abilities he developed in the Beckwith lifetime as that lifetime was full of struggle and pain.

In addition to the Beckwith lifetime, a prior incarnation for Captain Snow has been identified through Ahtun Re. Snow was Gabriel Nicolas de La Reynie, Chief of Police in Paris during the reign of Louis XIV, and principle investigator in the famous murder scandal known as the Affair of the Poisons. I knew de La Reynie in that era as I had a past incarnation as Jean-Baptiste Colbert, an economics minister to Louis XIV. If these French cases are accepted, then this is a good example of how souls who worked together in the past under the administration of Louis XIV have returned to work together again, though on a different project, this time involving reincarnation.

In addition, if these cases are valid, observe that in two lifetimes Robert Snow has served as a chief or captain of police, roles which appear to be comfortable for him. It is interesting to note that Snow was an honors student in college, scoring all top marks, and he received a scholarship to complete a doctorate in psychology. However, he abandoned his studies to become a policeman. Leadership in police work seems to be a calling.

Even in his lifetime as an artist, Snow demonstrated leadership and administrative skills, as Carroll Beckwith became the President of the New York Academy of Design. Thus, in three lifetimes, the traits of leadership and organizational skill are observed. In the lifetime of Beckwith, the soul of Captain Snow was able to follow a different career path and express a different energy or skill, the Fourth Ray energy of the artist, if we use the model of the Seven Rays. Captain Snow's more dominant energy, however, seems to be the First Ray, the energy of leadership and will, which is naturally expressed in his role of chief or captain of police.

Nicholas de Le Reynie **Carroll Beckwith** **Robert Snow**

Detail Carroll Beckwith, Self Portrait, 1898 James Carroll Beckwith. Gift of the Artist, Photograph © 1999 The Detroit Institute of the Arts.

8

Stages of Human Evolution and Karma

In the chapters of this book, we have discussed the process of creation, noting that God created monads and souls just after the Big Bang. The monad, the aspect of us that remains with God, acts like a prism that separates God's white light into a unique energy spectrum that is transmitted to the soul. The soul is an energetic body that is the storehouse of our experiences. To describe the relationship between the monad and the soul, we used the analogy of a yo-yo, where the round body of the yo-yo is the soul that is connected to the monad by an energetic string called the antakarana in Hindu philosophy.

The soul, we have described, is able to project holograms of itself onto the physical plane, into physical bodies, which become imbued with the qualities of the soul. The energy template that the soul projects into the physical body creates our characteristic appearance. Our energy spectrum, as well as our past-life experiences, are reflected in our personality. We can imagine the antakarana as also connecting the soul with the energetic hologram that it projects into the physical body. Thus, this energetic string runs from the monad to the soul to the body.

We have explored several models of personality, such as the Seven Rays, the archetypes of astrology, the Kabbalah and the Enneagram, to better understand our energy spectrum. We have also reviewed how our energy spectrum is expressed in a particular incarnation can be modified by genetic, biological, social and karmic factors.

At this point, I would like to review the history of the soul's evolution as described by two of Kevin Ryerson's spirit guides – John, who identifies himself as the Apostle John of the New Testament, and Ahtun Re, the Egyptian spirit guide who has demonstrated an ability to make accurate past-life matches. Ahtun Re, recall, has not incarnated in over 3,000 years. From the spirit realm, he has made human evolution an object of study and he relates that he has served as a spirit guide to teachers like Jesus. As Kevin Ryerson, the channel for these guides, was raised in the United States in the context of the Judeo-Christian culture, and because of John's incarnation in association with Jesus, references to biblical themes are used to describe the process of human evolution.

Innocents

In the scheme of things, Ahtun Re relates that after the creation of monads and souls, souls were one with God. He has referred to these new souls as "innocents." Though these souls were one with God and at peace, Ahtun Re has noted, "You can only be an innocent for so long." Just as in the course of a human life, one can be a child for only a limited period of time, souls had to leave the lap of God to establish individual identities. Reflect on how a child has to leave home and go to school to develop and grow, to become a mature human being. So too, souls had to leave the nest and experience creation to gain identity.

The Fall from Paradise

God sent out souls, not only to experience creation, according to John and Ahtun Re, but also to help diversify creation. They state that souls were sent by God to different parts of the universe and that a relatively small percentage of all created souls came to Earth. God's intention was that these souls tend to the Earth and its developing life forms from a spiritual perspective, much as we imagine that angels exist in the spirit planes that help human beings.

If we return to our concept that the soul can project energetic holograms, holograms would have been used to help direct the evolution of biological life. In their association with Earth life, though, souls became so enamored with the experiences of biological life that they became immersed in it. Souls began projecting their consciousness, began incarnating, into biological life, which apparently was not part of the original plan.

To better understand what happened, let us use the analogy of a farm. Let us say that God created a farm with animals and crops and he told his children, new souls, to tend to the farm. The intent was for these souls to tend to creation from the spirit planes, to help diversify creation through energetic interventions. Souls, however, became so fascinated with the creatures of the Earth that souls merged, placed their consciousness into the creatures of creation.

Souls for a period of time did incarnate into animal forms, which is the basis of the Hindu belief that a human soul can incarnate into animals such as cows. This experience with animal forms is also the basis of certain affinities that we have for particular animals or species. For example, those who have a great love of birds may have experienced incarnating into the bird kingdom.

The Christian Church Father Synesius (373–414 CE), Bishop of Ptolemais, speculated on the possibility that human souls once incarnated into animals. In his *Treatise on Dreams,* he wrote, "Philosophy speaks of souls being prepared by a course of transmigrations ... When first it comes down to Earth, it (the soul) embarks on this animal spirit as on a boat, and through it is brought into contact with matter."[1] Though Ahtun Re supports that incarnation into animal forms did represent a stage in the evolution of human souls, this happened eons ago and no longer occurs. Humans, at least while incarnating on planet Earth, reincarnate only as humans.

An unanticipated consequence of becoming immersed in biological life, though, was that a conscious connection with God and the spirit world was lost. The analogy of the vine comes to mind, in which all individual leaves on a vine are interconnected through the vine. Imagine that God is the vine and that we are the leaves. By incarnating into physical form, souls became separated from the vine, like leaves that have fallen from their stems.

In their forays into physical form, souls developed a karmic imprint that recorded their deeds and actions while in physical form. Though God gave souls free will and did not interfere with choices made, God did create the universe with certain laws and systems, one of which is the law of karma. What a soul does to another soul must be equalized on the same plane of existence on which the action occurred. As souls incurred karma on the physical plane, these souls had to return to the Earth plane to neutralize karma incurred in prior existences on Earth.

We can understand the biblical story of Adam and Eve through this process of incarnating into biological life. The tasting of the apple, the fruit of knowledge, and the subsequent expulsion from the Garden of Eden can be seen as an allegory of what happened as souls used their free will to incarnate into physical form. Souls gained the knowledge of what it was like to incarnate physically, but in the process, humanity lost the experience of paradise where they had been consciously connected with God.

Let us turn to our yo-yo analogy to visualize what happened. Imagine that the monad exists at the Godhead, while the soul, the seat of consciousness, descends on its string through the lower planes of existence, planes that will be described in pages that follow. Souls who became human descended all the way down to Earth's dense physical plane, incarnating into physical, biological forms. In descending so deeply, imagine that our yo-yos got stuck in the mud of Earthly existence and could no longer rebound to the higher planes. Conscious connections to God and the higher spiritual planes were lost during incarnation on Earth. Further, the soul, though outside physical form, was caught in, or restricted to, the lower spiritual planes as well.

To rectify this situation, according to Kevin's guides John and Ahtun Re, spirit beings who were charged with supervising the evolution of souls determined that consciousness could be raised utilizing primate animal forms for incarnation. Applying energetic templates, higher spirit beings, with the help of God, helped primates evolve into *Homo sapiens*. Thus, the human being, in the form of *Homo sapiens,* was created to help souls evolve more quickly on the Earth plane.

By incarnating into the form of *Homo sapiens* and by utilizing mind and reason, human souls would be able to reach higher spiritual dimensions once again and the connection with God could be reestablished. Interestingly, in this way, biological evolution and Creationism can be reconciled. Evolution does proceed as a gradual process as biology proposes, but just as the soul can project an energy template of itself into the physical form which results in facial features appearing consistent from one incarnation to another, spirit beings can influence biological evolution through energetic interventions.

What was the consequence of the Fall, the loss of connection to God due to incarnation into the dense physical plane? One negative consequence is man's inhumanity to man, for if humanity had retained its connection to the higher planes and with God, human beings could not be cruel to one another. Had we remained connected to the higher planes, we would know that the differences that separate us, be they race, religion, ethnic or national differences, which, historically, have been the causes of human conflict, are artificial differences. We would also know that the pain we cause others will come back to us though the law of karma.

The loss of connection with God is the reason life is filled with so much hardship. This is why students of the metaphysical work, *A Course in Miracles,* state that this world is not of God's making but of man's making, and that one must reject the trappings of Earthly existence for God's universe.

The message of *A Course in Miracles* is being popularized through Gary Renard and his book *Disappearance of the Universe.* By choosing to forgive others, one will be freed of karmic bonds and eventually perceive higher worlds. In this process, through an opening of clairvoyance, the physical world disappears and higher spiritual realms appear. This indeed, was the great mission of Jesus of Nazareth, to teach people to choose God's kingdom over man's kingdom, to attain the higher spiritual planes through forgiveness and love.

One may also take a different view of the Fall. Some view man's incursion into dense physical matter as an experiment, which in the end may allow souls to develop more effectively. Using the yo-yo analogy, once the soul frees itself from the mud, it may boomerang back to its source with a greater range of experience. When I asked Ahtun Re whether this was true, whether the descent into dense form was a conscious experiment, Ahtun Re related that this point of view can be held as valid. He indicated that the Fall could be viewed as an experiment in which souls said, "Let's see what happens if we move all the way down into physical matter."

The positive aspect of this experiment is that human souls gain experience with matter and, according to Ahtun Re, will ultimately become more powerful and effective co-creators with God. In the future, when new worlds are born, souls that went through Earthly incarnation will be better able to assist in the new creation. Just as one cannot fly a jumbo jet without logging many hours in smaller aircraft, incarnation on Earth is a training ground for learning about matter and biological life, experiencing instincts and emotions, and gaining mastery in functioning in physical matter.

In contrast, Ahtun Re remarked, angels have never incarnated into physical matter and they fear incarnating on Earth. Though angels have not had to struggle with the demands of Earthly incarnation, such as the need to survive in a physical body and to deal with disease or death, they also have not had the range of experience that human souls possess.

In the end, the trials of existence on Earth make us more versatile and capable in the spirit realms. Though we may be bound to incarnate on Earth for a period of time due to our depth of incursion into the physical, Ahtun Re has pointed out that if it takes a human being a few thousand years or even a million years longer to return to Source, to God, this is not a big concern, for a million years to the soul is nothing.

The greatest tragedy, as mentioned, of incarnating so deeply into matter is that the loss of conscious connection with the higher spiritual planes has ultimately led to man's inhumanity to man. Loss of the conscious knowledge that we reincarnate and can change religion, nationality, race and gender from one incarnation to another has caused separation and conflict based on differences in these affiliations.

On Earth, we have become separated souls, based on the social and religious affiliations that we identify with, rather than remaining universal souls, which is our true nature. If we, as the human race, collectively and consciously evolve more quickly, then suffering and conflict on Earth will end sooner. In turn, providing objective evidence of reincarnation can serve as a catalyst to accelerate human spiritual evolution. This, I believe, is a worthy goal.

Stages of Evolution

Let us now review and expand upon the stages in the development of the soul as described by Ahtun Re.

First Stage: Innocents

New souls, just budded off from God, represent the first stage of evolution. These souls were created about 14 billion years ago just after the Big Bang. This stage precedes incarnation.

Second Stage: Orphans

In paragraphs above, it was described how souls were sent to Earth to help diversify creation. Using energetic templates, spirit beings helped create the building blocks of life, such as self-replicating DNA-like molecules. Spirit beings participated in the creation of early plants and organisms, which eventually evolved into the ecosystem we now know. When animal life evolved, human souls decided to incarnate deeply into physical form, which led to a pattern of incarnation in which conscious connection to the spirit world was lost. This loss of connection by incarnate souls led to the fear of death and confusion about the purpose of life.

The human being in the orphan stage is driven by survival needs and much violent behavior is observed. In this stage, human beings incur a great deal of negative karma by harming one another. One cause of the violence is that in incarnating into an animal-based, physical form, a soul on Earth is imbued with animal instincts, including the drive to survive, territoriality and identification with one's clan or group. This, in combination with the loss of conscious connection with the spiritual world and with God, leads to violent acts.

Third Stage: Warrior/Statesman

Human beings eventually developed societies and a social conscience. Religious doctrines evolved that provided people much comfort, as both a meaning to life and survival after death were promised in these doctrines. Societies developed identities through their religious and social customs. Human beings became identified with their social structures, their nationalities, religions and ethic affiliations.

Indeed, the greatest power that organized religions have is that they offer solace and escape from one of man's greatest fears, the fear of annihilation. Problems arise, though, when different religions come into conflict with one another. This conflict can cause great anxiety, for the individual understands that conflicting religious doctrines can't logically all be right.

Violence between religious groups stems from the need for one's religion to prevail, for ultimately, one's religion provides a place for the individual in heaven. It is even rationalized that it is acceptable to kill other human beings in the name of religion. Ahtun Re has termed this the "warrior" stage, where individuals will die to protect a particular religious doctrine, a particular religious truth – a truth, Ahtun Re adds, that doesn't need protecting.

Identification with other social groups, such as nationalities or ethnic groups, also leads to separation and conflict. These violent conflicts serve only to promote continuing cycles of violence: souls reincarnate harboring wounds, which lead to acts of revenge. Ironically, souls can reincarnate into the groups they previously fought: Christian Crusaders can reincarnate as Muslims, Muslims can reincarnate as Hindus or Jews, and so on. Over time, man's inhumanity to man has led to ongoing karmic cycles of violence that continue up to this day.

Stage Four: The Wanderer/Philosopher

The next stage is that of the wanderer, who seeks to reestablish a conscious connection with God and the spirit world. The wanderer surveys philosophies and spiritual systems, assimilating truths. In this stage, practices such as meditation may be implemented. The wanderer looks for universal truths.

Stage Five: The Healer/Sage

The last stage of human evolution, according to Ahtun Re, is the stage of the healer or sage, who understands that we are all universal souls that are one with God. Through multiple incarnations, the healer or sage develops the innate knowledge that the soul is eternal and that divisions between people based on religion, race, ethnic origin and gender are baseless. The healer or sage strives to create a more peaceful and compassionate world.

Cycles of Violence, Human Evolution and Free Will

A question often asked is why did God create a world that is filled with so much conflict and suffering? The answer goes back to the issue of free will. Ahtun Re once quipped, "God created a perfect universe, but the kids screwed it up." Like rebellious adolescents, humanity chose through free will to enter deeply into physical form, which resulted in the severing of our conscious connection with God, which led to our forgetting our oneness with God and each other, which has led to karmic cycles of violence. We also have free will, though, to end the cycles of violence and restore our conscious connection to God and with each other.

How to break cycles of karma is the focus of the metaphysical work mentioned previously, *A Course in Miracles,* as well as Gary Renard's books *Disappearance of the Universe* and *Your Immortal Reality,* which are based on the *Course.* The *Course* emphasizes that our Earth existence is not the real world.

The *Course* teaches by hyperbole, by pushing a point to its limit, and by gentle exaggeration. By stating that the world is not real, the *Course* alludes to the idea that human souls, through free will, contributed to how this world evolved, and that this world is not God's world, the real world. The key to reentering God's world, the spirit world, is to reestablish one's connection to God. This involves breaking cycles of karma. The way to do this is through forgiveness.

It is my belief that objective evidence of reincarnation, which will inevitably grow with time, will help humanity as a whole to break the cycles of violence. First of all, evidence of reincarnation allays the fear that our existence ends when we die. Reincarnation cases presented in *Born Again* and *Return of the Revolutionaries* demonstrate that we reincarnate in personas very much like the ones we were before. Further, we reincarnate with the ones we have loved and cared for in past incarnations. This evidence diminishes the need to have strict religious doctrines to rely on to reassure us that we will survive death and gain entrance into the spirit world, into heaven.

With objective evidence of reincarnation and an increased understanding of spiritual evolution, the orphan doesn't have to be afraid, the warrior no longer has to fight to protect a religious or political truth, and the wanderer no longer has to search. From this point forward, we can all move to the stage that Ahtun Re terms the healer. Perhaps the epitome of a healer is found in the figure of Jesus, who urged that we love God and each other. Just as we, the evolutionary lineage that we call humanity, used free will to become separated from God, we can use free will to reconnect with God and each other.

Why the Broad Range of Levels of Development?

One thing that has puzzled me is why there is such diversity in the levels of soul development if all souls were created at the same time. Why are we not more uniform in spiritual development? On any television news program, as in any newspaper, we are shown extremes of human behavior, from great humanitarians who sacrifice their lives for others to child molesters and murderers.

I asked Ahtun Re this question and his reply was that God gave souls free will to develop at their own rate. He pointed out that a soul can decide not to incarnate for thousands or millions of years, which also means that the soul will not develop much in that interval. Sooner or later, the urge, the desire to evolve will kick in, and the soul will enter the physical plane in the orphan stage while other souls have already advanced to higher levels.

Why is Earth Incarnation Necessary?

Though we have discussed how different degrees of incursion were possible and that humanity chose to incarnate deeply onto the physical plane, some form of incarnation is required, for a period of time, as incarnation demonstrates who we really are. Ahtun Re makes the comparison of a doctor in training who goes through medical school. Upon graduation, the doctor has knowledge, but has not demonstrated this knowledge in application. The graduate has to practice medicine to really become a physician, to gain the skills and identity of a physician.

In the same way, in the spirit world, we can learn and absorb knowledge, we can believe that we are of a certain level of maturity, but for us to really know ourselves, we must incarnate to demonstrate who we are. The physical plane is not only a place where we gain experience and identity; it is also a proving ground.

On the positive side, one can look at incarnation on Earth as an opportunity to do spiritual weight-lifting. The autonomy that Earthly incarnation brings with it, where most of us are disconnected from the spirit world, forces us to exert ourselves, to develop strength, endurance, knowledge and wisdom. Some consider being human to be a great privilege, as the growth that can be attained through human incarnation is much more substantial than can be attained through other lines of spiritual development.

Why Can't We Remember Past Lives?

We have noted that by incarnating deeply into physical existence, humanity lost its connection to the spirit world. A different though related question is: why can't we remember past lives? One of the primary reasons is that if we remembered all our lives and all the hurts and grievances associated with past lives, we couldn't be productive in our current lives, nor would we establish relationships with others with whom we have karmic issues and lessons.

In my book, *Return of the Revolutionaries,* I present the case of my ex-wife, Oksana, who is identified as the reincarnation of my son, Charles Adams, in a prior lifetime during the American Revolution. In *Revolutionaries,* I am identified as the reincarnation of John Adams. In that era, Charles and I had a tempestuous relationship and in the end, I cut off all communication with him. Both Charles and I had wounds from that relationship.

The way that karma works is that through reincarnation, we are brought back together with those with whom we have issues to resolve. As mentioned, Charles reincarnated in contemporary times as my ex-wife Oksana. We were guided back together by destiny and fell in love with each other immediately. We were married within six months. Though eventually we divorced, we had the opportunity through marriage to truly get to know and love one another, an opportunity we didn't have to the same extent in our prior lifetimes.

What do you think would have happened, though, if both Oksana and I had known about our past-life relationship when we met – had known that Oksana was my son Charles 200 years ago, and that we had bad karma to work out between us? We both would likely have run in opposite directions! Indeed, I was not made aware of our past-life relationship until a year after we had separated.

Another reason people don't remember past lives is that we would have to relive traumatic deaths. Even when such deaths are not consciously remembered, they can result in phobias or other psychological conditions in subsequent lifetimes. In *Revolutionaries,* I describe that a past life was derived for a woman named Michelle. Through the reincarnation research that I was doing, Michelle was identified as my granddaughter in the same lifetime in which Oksana was my son. The granddaughter had died when a boat that she was on in the Hudson River caught fire and sank.

When I told Michelle about the hypothesized past lifetime, she revealed that she has had a lifelong fear of boats and open water, a fact that I was not aware of when the past-life match for her was derived. Often times, though not always, when a person becomes aware of such a traumatic event in a prior incarnation, as can occur through past-life regression, the phobia will subside.

It can work the other way too. If one becomes aware of a past lifetime in which a friend betrayed or hurt them, and that friend has reincarnated once again in one's circle, then the wound from the past lifetime can be reopened in contemporary times. Life is tough enough dealing with hurts incurred this time round. Dealing with wounds from prior lifetimes makes thing all the more difficult. Indeed, traditional psychotherapy may be needed to deal with wounds that resurface from past lives.

Eventually, as we develop into the stages of wanderer and sage, we may retrieve past-life information, but for the reasons described above, such information is blocked until we are mature enough to deal with it. For example, orphan souls, if given past-life information about someone who hurt them in a past lifetime, may act out and try to physically harm the reincarnated person in contemporary times. Often, even without specific memories, aggressive behavior towards others is related to emotions and resentments associated with past incarnations.

Dealing with Karma

Karma is traditionally seen as the law of cause and effect, in which an action will result in a reciprocal effect. With positive karma, if you perform a good act for someone, that good will return to you in a subsequent time. With negative karma, if you harm someone in one lifetime, then that harm will return to you. There are two basic ways that negative karma can be dealt with: in a retributive way or in a transformational way.

Let us use the example of gang violence. Let us say that one gang member, whom we call the perpetrator, kills another. In between lifetimes, let us say that the perpetrator experiences no remorse over the killing. In a subsequent lifetime, the perpetrator, if he or she reincarnates with the same mentality, would need to experience being murdered or having a loved one murdered to experience first-hand the loss that occurs through violence.

On the other hand, let us imagine that in between incarnations the perpetrator experiences great remorse for the murder. The perpetrator again reincarnates in a gang setting, but develops increased maturity and conscious awareness through reflection and effort. The perpetrator may even renounce gang violence. He or she may work with young people this time around to prevent gang violence. Instead of having to experience being murdered, the perpetrator, in acting as a healer, can transform karma in a positive way. It is through reflection and effort that the orphan soul can move into higher stages of development.

This is why the message that Jesus gave regarding the importance of forgiveness is so profound. By hanging on to resentments, by insisting that karma be enforced in a retributive, eye-for-an-eye manner, we lock ourselves into lower levels of spiritual development. We remain orphans or warriors. Cycles of violence are perpetuated. But if we forgive others, then we are freed from retributive karma. Karma can be played out in a more transformative way and the individual progresses to the stage of the wanderer, the healer, the sage.

9

Levels of the Spiritual World

Describing and defining the landscape of the spiritual world will be a tapestry woven over time. I am not clairvoyant and do not have the ability to perceive these realms, so I must rely on the observations of others. Two individuals who do write about their experiences in the spirit world include professional clairvoyants Echo Bodine and Judy Goodman.

Echo, in her book, *Echoes of the Soul,* describes the equivalent of a near-death experience which she undertook voluntarily and consciously to bring back information about the spirit world to humanity. Judy Goodman relates that she has the ability to travel to the spiritual realms at will and indeed, Judy states that she lives in the physical world and spirit world simultaneously. Echo and Judy both describe seven levels that make up the spiritual world, which is consistent with concepts advanced by Theosophy.

I have also used Ahtun Re, the spirit guide that Kevin Ryerson channels, who has demonstrated an ability to make accurate past-life matches. I felt that Ahtun Re would be another good resource since, after all, he lives in the spirit world, not having incarnated for over 3,000 years.

Ahtun Re has told me that there are twelve dimensions or levels in the spirit world, seven which have been described through human experience, and another five dimensions known only to those in the spirit world. He has explained that the human experience of the spirit world is conditioned by the seven chakras, which are energy centers that run from the base of the spine to the crown of the head. Ahtun Re has explained that since we are conditioned by the seven chakras, humanity can only be aware of the seven planes of the spirit world that correspond to the seven chakras.

At this point, I would like to share that when I took a psychic development class years ago, I was very definitely able to feel the chakras as I ran my hand up and down a foot or so in front of other students in the class. I felt a gentle pressure or energy against my hand as it passed in front a person's chakra. Though in my opinion, I was the least clairvoyantly gifted in the class, I was able to feel the chakras.

In a session with Kevin Ryerson, I asked Ahtun Re what his existence is like in the spirit world. Ahtun Re stated that he exists on the 11th and 12th dimensions, near the Godhead. He relates that in the 12th dimension, his individual identity fades and he is conscious only of being one with God. He describes this experience as being in a state of "lucid ecstasy." I suppose this is why, whenever I have sessions Kevin, Ahtun Re always seems to be in a very good mood.

Ahtun Re further relates that when he drops down to the 11th dimension, his sense of individuality returns. His experience in the 11th dimension is one of a holographic reality where he can create scenes at will. When he communicates with human beings, as when individuals have sessions with Kevin, Ahtun Re creates an Egyptian temple, as he still has a great fondness for his past incarnations in Egypt.

In my sessions with Kevin, Ahtun Re describes that in the holographic Egyptian temple that he creates on the 11th plane, I appear in the attire of an Egyptian priest. Ahtun Re says that the garb I wear reflects the level of my current spiritual achievement. I have been afraid to ask Ahtun Re what that level is, so I cannot comment further on my garb. During a telephone session with Kevin, while I am furiously taking notes on my kitchen table in San Francisco, Ahtun Re perceives me scribing on a table in his Egyptian temple.

In my perception, Ahtun Re is indeed a very highly evolved spirit being, one who can be seen as representing the endpoint that we all will eventually want to attain, the state of being where we can merge with God on the spiritual plane, yet who can also project consciousness into the dense plane of Earthly existence. In other words, Ahtun Re's yo-yo can go all the way down to the physical plane and all the way back up to the Godhead.

As a testament to his abilities, when Kevin Ryerson leads travel groups to Machu Picchu in Peru, Ahtun Re is known to take control of Kevin's body. While Kevin is blindfolded, Ahtun Re will then walk Kevin's body along a narrow trail on a cliff's edge. What is impressive is that Kevin is still with us!

Another person who alluded to the ability to span the planes is Jesus, as demonstrated by statements he made like "I and the Father are one" and "In my Father's house are many mansions."

Let us now review the spiritual planes as reported by Echo Bodine and Judy Goodman. We will start with Echo, who has documented her experiences in her book, *Echoes of the Soul.* I thank Echo for allowing me to share her work with you. Her story starts humorously, as she describes how she learned of latent psychic abilities that she and other family members possessed.

Echo Travels to Heaven

Echo relates that when she was 17 years old, in the fall of 1965 in Minnesota, she was with her family at their dinner table. They were talking and listening to Michael, Echo's younger brother, practicing on his drum set in the basement of their home. Echo relates that her brother was a beginner, which would imply that his playing was just a shade better than noise. Suddenly, the noise ended and beautiful, sophisticated drumming rang out in the house. Echo's family members didn't understand what had happened and hypothesized that recorded drum music was being played. What else could it be?

The music then stopped and Echo's very frightened brother ran up the stairs. Michael stated that as he was practicing with eyes closed, he saw a white ghost-like figure float over to him. The ghost-like being took his hands and began drumming, which resulted in the sophisticated rhythms that the family had heard. After playing for a while, the white figure let go and floated away.

Hoping to understand what had happened, Echo's mother called Eve Olson, a medium she knew through her prayer group. Eve told the family that the white figure was a spirit guide of her brother's who was a professional drummer in a past lifetime. In addition to her brother having the ability to perceive that spirit drummer, Eve said that Echo had four of the psychic gifts – clairvoyance (seeing visions), clairaudience (hearing spirit), clairsentience (the gift of psychic sensing or feeling) and clairalience (the gift of psychic smell) – as well as the gift of healing.

Eve said that in past incarnations, Echo had helped found mystery schools and that she would write several books in this lifetime. Eve also said that Echo would be on radio and television and that she would travel throughout the world teaching others how to develop their spiritual gifts.

At the time, Echo had no conscious knowledge of these abilities. Having grown up in a family with two alcoholic parents, all she wanted to do was to become a social worker and have a normal life with a husband and children. Nonetheless, as time went on, Eve's predictions about Echo came true. Eve further stated that Michael, Echo's brother, was also psychically gifted and this prediction turned out to be true as well.

Twelve years later, Echo was working as a professional psychic and she also took jobs, with help from her brother Michael, as a "ghostbuster," helping spirits who were attached to the Earth move on to higher realms. By 1992, Echo had done ghostbusting work for about fifteen years, and it occurred to her that it would be helpful for her to know more about the spiritual realms where she was sending the ghosts. Echo prayed to God, asking if she could learn more about the other side.

Three days later, while she was in her office with a client, a hazy white light began to fill the room. A blonde female spirit guide appeared and said to Echo, "Let's go, let's go." Echo, feeling disoriented by the experience, asked her client to telephone her brother

Michael and ask him to come help her through what was to come. On his way to Echo's office, Michael related that his spirit guides, three days earlier, had told him that Echo had asked God that she be shown the other side. Michael's guides had also informed him that Echo would travel to the other side and that he needed to hold her hand to ground her physically while her soul was out of her body.

As soon as Michael arrived and took Echo's hand, the blonde apparition turned around, looked Echo right in the eye and said, "Let's go." It was then that Echo realized that this blond spirit guide was her own soul. Echo then immediately shot out of her body and found herself in a tunnel. She felt a loving, warm energy pull her deeper into the tunnel towards a white light. Echo saw many reunions taking place within the tunnel, souls who were departing from the Earth plane who were being greeted by deceased friends and relatives.

When she came out of the tunnel, Echo saw a quaint village with cobblestone streets. Her grandmother was standing there with a friend who said to the grandmother, "You didn't tell me that she was dying today." Echo's grandmother responded, "Oh no, she's not dying, just visiting." Echo noted that her grandmother had the same facial features as when she was on Earth and that she looked so young, beautiful and alive. Echo observed that several of her grandmother's friends who had died were around her.

Suddenly, an angel appeared who announced to Echo that she would be her guide. The first place the angel took her to was called the Pink Place, which was a community that had a pink aura around it. There was a hospital-like structure in the Pink Place, where caregivers were assisting souls who were having difficulty accepting their death. Echo also noted that souls who had had physically handicapped bodies on Earth were being helped in adjusting to healthy and complete spirit bodies. One section of the hospital was for suicide victims who were being assisted in processing their transitions.

The angel told Echo that the Pink Place was for healing. Echo observed hundreds of souls lying in the grass with their eyes closed, receiving healing from the energy in the community. Echo and the angel then floated across an amazing landscape, surrounded by every possible kind of flower and tree.

Next, they came to a white and gold coliseum with enormous pillars, huge windows and doors that were always open. The angel told Echo that this was where angels live who help people on Earth. Next, they floated to a meadow filled with musicians and singers. Several types of music were being played, and by tuning into a particular vibration, Echo could hear the music of her choosing.

The next part of the tour was especially significant for Echo. The angel took her to a magnificent nature scene where thousands of souls were milling around. In the center was a man speaking and teaching who captivated the crowd. Echo knew intuitively that the man she was staring at was Jesus, but she couldn't believe that she was allowed to be in what felt like such a sacred place. She asked who this man was, and the angel told her that it was indeed Jesus and that this magnificent place was called the City of Jesus. Jesus has always been a central figure in Echo's life and the angel wanted her to see him in the spiritual realm. Echo describes that his whole essence was love, but that she could also feel his power, gentleness and sense of humor.

Echo then heard her brother Michael telling her to look for God. As she looked around, she realized that she was surrounded by God, that God was everywhere, that God was a presence, a knowingness that was difficult to describe.

The angel told Echo that heaven was full of communities and that each reflected a different reality. She said that the reality we live by on Earth, the consciousness that we hold, determines where we go in heaven. For example, if one was a hard-working, devout Catholic, then in heaven that person would live in a community that embraces those same values and beliefs. The angel then showed Echo a community of beggars and thieves, who all day long steal or beg from one another.

The angel related that there is a community on the other side that is similar to a hell, but she quickly clarified that it is we who created this community because of our belief systems, and not God.

She adamantly stated that God would never create a hell nor would God send any of his children to such a place. She said many people believe that they will go to hell because of their negative actions throughout their life, so they actually seek this community out because of their beliefs. At some point, all souls will realize that they have created this place, not God, and then this community will no longer exist, just as the community of beggars and thieves will no longer exist when souls there realize that there is a better way to live.

The angel told Echo that each community in heaven has a classroom with an instructor who helps souls to learn, grow and evolve. Echo, being a movie buff, asked where the movie stars lived. The angel told her that they have their own community, but that they don't have to live there. If they are ready to let go of who they were when living on Earth and move on, they live in other communities that reflect their beliefs and level of consciousness or development.

Echo could hear Michael telling her that she needed to get back to her body, but she did not want to go back. She really wanted to stay in heaven, but both Michael and the angel told her she needed to leave and get back. The angel looked her right in the eye and told her that she was not allowed to take this journey just for her own sake, that she had been given this tour so that she could share this information with as many people as possible and help them heal their fear of death. Then, out of the corner of her right eye, Echo noted a broad staircase. Curious, she asked the angel where the stairway led. The angel explained that there are several levels to heaven and that the highest level is where we all experience the same reality, where we know that we are all one with God.

Before Echo went back to her body, she asked the angel one last question. Was the village with cobblestones, the place where she had started her journey, the entrance to heaven? The angel responded that there were many places throughout heaven where people arrived. For example, some arriving souls go directly to the Pink Place hospital. Others go to other entry points that were determined by their level of consciousness.

After that, Echo shot back to her body and upon regaining awareness of the physical world, found herself exhausted. Her body was like a rag doll, lifeless and limp, and it was twenty minutes before she could speak. An hour passed before she felt normal and when she went to bed, Echo slept for twelve hours.

Following her journey to the spiritual realm in 1992, Echo's ability to travel to the spiritual world has become stronger. From her experiences, she has categorized the spiritual planes into seven levels, with the highest level being that of being one with God. Beings gravitate to the level consistent with their development and consciousness. The seven levels according to Echo are described below:

Level 1: Souls on this plane are self-absorbed and unaware that there is a connection between all things. Their consciousness is focused on survival and they take what they want. Souls on this level experience fear. Though these souls have a conscience, an inner voice that tells of right and wrong, they ignore this voice, believing that karma doesn't apply to them. But in actual fact, it is where the whole cycle of karma begins. In Ahtun Re's model of soul development, this level would the home of orphan souls.

Level 2: Echo relates that on this plane, souls slowly begin to open their hearts to other people and animals, but their level of trust is still quite low. They begin to see that possibly not everyone is out to get them and that there might be good in the world, as well as all the bad that they were so aware of as a level one soul. They go back and forth between trying to trust and not trusting and, unfortunately, can continue to create some pretty negative karma for themselves. They will often get involved in religions that teach about hell and damnation and that are based on shame and guilt. Souls can get very stuck in this pattern for many lifetimes.

Level 3: Souls on this level have learned (through some tough karmic lessons) the difference between right and wrong. They feel a desire to change the way they think and feel and relate to the world. They see more of the positive possibilities rather than the negative. Level three souls start to sense that there is more to them than what religion has taught them. They search for truth within safe boundaries. Souls begin to understand the law of karma and begin to realize that they are accountable for their actions. Souls on this plane still have fears regarding survival and other souls, but more and more, they see the similarities between people rather than the differences.

Level 4: Souls at this level strive to understand oneness with all living beings and God, moving from religious orientations to more universal and spiritual philosophies. In physical existence, souls on this level question more, read books and pursue a spiritual quest. Material attachments and physical cravings are lessened and wisdom is sought in life lessons. Echo notes that level four souls still have karma, can grieve and still go through the process of reincarnation.

Level 5: Echo describes Level 5 as the beginning of Nirvana, where souls understand abundance, know of their partnership with God, and have a feeling of responsibility for the whole of humanity. Souls no longer blame God or others. Immaturity, demonstrated by competition or rebelliousness, has been overcome. There are no feelings of lack or limitation, and there is no more grieving. The settings in this level are beautiful, with lush nature scenes. There is a feeling of love, calmness and serenity. There is a fluid-like quality to existence, though there is also intensity. Echo relates that level five souls know how draining Earth life can be for the soul, and they help teach souls on Level 4 how not to have to reincarnate. Level five souls are like angels who have given up attachments on Earth and are looking forward to "retirement" on higher levels, closer to the consciousness of God.

Ahtun Re, by the way, has indicated that Jesus came from Level 5 when he began his ministry 2,000 years ago and that he has since transitioned into higher realms.

Level 6: Echo relates that at this level, souls have gone deeper into the heart of God, knowing God more fully. Level six souls live in a blissful state, and she notes that there is nothing like it on Earth.

Level 7: On this plane, Echo describes souls as Godlike, as they are one with God and all other souls. Echo notes that souls at this level have attained retirement in the truest sense.

Once again, I thank Echo for allowing me to share her journey with you. You can learn more about Echo and her work at: www.echo bodine.com

At this point, I would like to share the experiences of Judy Goodman, a clairvoyant and spiritual teacher who also can travel through the spiritual planes. As noted previously, Judy relates that she can live in the physical world and spiritual world simultaneously. Judy has written the narrative provided below and I thank her for this contribution. Judy's description of the spiritual realms is compatible with Echo's, though there are some differences.

The angel who guided Echo noted that there are many portals to heaven and that there are many different communities at every level of the spiritual world, consistent with the statement of Jesus, "My Father's house has many mansions." As such, it would be expected that different travelers to the spiritual world have different experiences and perceptions. Let us now turn to Judy's narrative.

Judy Goodman: Dynamics of the Spiritual World

I want to discuss some of the dynamics of "the other side," but before I do, let me make a few points very clear. Whatever your belief system dictates, whatever your religion has taught you to expect at the time of your death, no matter what theory you embrace, it is exactly what your experience will be. While there are various levels of growth and experience on "the other side," within each level will be your own experience, which in turn relates directly to your spiritual needs.

Perhaps this personal story will help you understand this point. My father's mother was a deeply religious woman; her church was a central part of her entire life. Her belief system was very strong and clear-cut as to what her "after life" would be like. Since my birth, I have walked in both the physical and spirit world. This allows me to check in on situations and have a better understanding of what happens when our loved ones die. I was able to check in with my grandmother's crossing and see what her experience was like; it allowed me to know if she was okay.

As I watched my grandmother's crossing, she experienced exactly what her religious teachings had indicated would happen. She saw, felt and experienced everything that she grew up believing. She was greeted by family members and old friends. After she had rested and had had a chance to consider what was happening to her, she looked around, shook her head and said, "I can't believe I just did that."

At that point, she eased back into the knowledge that each of us has: she remembered who she really is. She had gone into the "light" and had an opportunity to review her life and all that it entailed. If she felt that she had made mistakes, she would have an opportunity to consider reincarnation as a way to make things right. If she had lived a good life and wanted to incarnate again and contribute to humanity, that too would be an option.

There are seven levels of growth on the other side, but there is never a "right" or "wrong" level of achievement when we return to the place from whence we came. Just as in our physical life, we each strive to achieve things from different perspectives. I believe you will agree that just because someone has become an important person in his lifetime, that does not mean he is "better" than other human beings are. Our growth, both physical and in spirit, seems to be a true example of the free will that we have had all along. No matter what level of spiritual growth you achieve, you are still equal to all others.

Level One: The Realm of New White Light

This realm contains new souls – those that have just crossed over. (This does not mean newly-created souls, just the ones that have just crossed back into spirit.) You will also find those that are waiting to go either way, either to the light or towards the vibration of darkness. Darkness will have no more power over you than you require, and will be based on your belief system and spiritual behavior. This space also serves as purgatory for those who embrace that in their religion. There is no punishment inflicted here, but sometimes the aimlessness of it all may feel just that way. Those who have not completely crossed over into the spirit realm, earthbound souls, will be at this level.

An earthbound soul will often stay in close proximity to the place it knew as home. Some will sleep here, perhaps for generations, and their energy may be used to help others. When energy is utilized in this space, it is not a self-sacrificing move, but simply utilization for the betterment of others. This usage of energy should not be confused with that of souls at a much higher level of work.

For those who have decided to reincarnate and are being prepared for their journey, preparation takes place here. Those who are reincarnating fairly soon will rarely go higher than this place. Most souls returning will forget all that they have ever been, all that they have ever known. Occasionally there will be some who return with all of their knowledge; these are the Teachers.

Life is an opportunity! Each experience will teach us something if we choose to accept that. Sometimes we wonder why things seem so tough, but we attract that which we need to in order to learn and grow. We choose the life we live and all that becomes a part of it! In some ways, life is like taking a test, and if we knew the answers ahead of time, why would we do the work? That is partially why, at our lower conscious level, we forget all the knowledge that we have. Our "higher self" will continue to be connected to the knowledge and the highest truth.

This is the busiest of all realms. For those who oversee this area, quick decision-making will be required. Angels abound in this place and travel to and from the Earth. Early tribal spirits and Angels do a great deal of the work here. There are numerous "Antiquities" in this realm. Antiquities provide a refuge for rest and whatever nourishment and emotional support the soul might require. At this level, the soul is not able to achieve these things on its own. These unique havens of safety hang in the dark part of the sky and look very much like stars; they cannot be moved or tampered with by a spirit that would control or harm others.

In this place, a soul does not have enough of its own strength to be independent. In many ways, you just go with the flow because you are not strong enough to do otherwise. At this level, you do not feel, smell or taste. Here we do not experience the behavior associated with a physical body but may be holding on to the mental or emotional pain of the past life. The soul is mostly transparent and sometimes not recognizable; we are spirit – not physical.

If we have lived a life that has caused pain and harm to others, if we have not cleared our issues before our death, the pain of our life review is multiplied seven times. When you were alive and had a physical body, your pain would have been distributed throughout the body. It could have become part of an illness or possibly the cause of your death. When you no longer have the physical body to hold the pain, the feelings and emotions are all that you have left. Even so, at all times we are given guidance and counsel to change and make things better for ourselves. On "the other side" time does not exist; a soul will not have an awareness of time required to make changes.

It is worth mentioning here that just because a person's life may have trauma in it, that does not mean that their passing will be painful or that their afterlife will be any less glorious than any other soul. The trauma of one's life is not the measurement of the soul. The true balance of our growth is based on more than one lifetime.

Level Two: The Realm of Angels and Protectors

We now begin to see beautiful homes, churches or places of celebration. Each of the buildings will be magnificent and reflective of almost every religion or belief system practiced on Earth and possibly in other universes.

When Angels choose to have a place of rest it will be here. It is not uncommon for them to travel within all levels of growth; they will frequently move between Level Two and Earth. It is not uncommon for them to sacrifice their "being" in order to help a soul. This is particularly true in the case of possession.

This is a place of peace and no harm will come to anyone here, but there is seldom contentment found. In most cases, the souls are always working – trying to help others. From this place there is great effort made to help those in Level One on the Earth; there is also extraordinary work for those that may be at the first level of an experience that some religious beliefs would describe as "hell." You may be surprised to learn that this experience, if you require it, has different levels too.

The Protectors here are of moderate strength and knowledge. They, too, still have many opportunities to grow and learn. Just because we cross back into spirit does not necessarily mean that we utilize our highest knowledge. In many cases, those that have gained permission to walk with us in body, do so as a way of learning and growing.

While it is wonderful to know that you do not walk alone, this is a good time to remind you to always use discernment when hearing the words of a "Protector," "Spirit Guide" or "Spiritual Advisor." The Creator did not create imperfect souls; within each of us is the answer to every question we will ask. There are "Protectors," "Teachers" and "Spirit Guides" that will come from other realms. No matter who walks with you, you must always make up your own mind because you are responsible for the choices you make. These great spirits will use their strength to help the weak and fearful. Once again, at this level, we find many "Antiquities" here to provide shelter and rest for those needing it.

Level Three: The Realm of Councils or Decision Makers

This is a very productive place and will be home to some that choose to do nothing at all. For those that choose the path of less involvement, somewhere they have earned the right to have this experience. It is not written anywhere that you must be busy at all times.

When a soul reaches this level and decides to "rest," it usually does not last long. You can live the perfect existence for only so long before you decide to get busy again. This is a place of magnificent homes, great facilities of knowledge, incredible gardens and a lot of authority.

Sometimes we will find souls that have not reincarnated for a very long time and may have lost touch with the needs of humanity. Usually these are members of a "Council." On occasion, there will be souls from Level Two that will come to work for the Councils. While this may make them seem as though they are in servitude, it is their way of growing and becoming much stronger. This is a sign of a great soul in the developmental process.

When a "Council" is comprised of members that have not reincarnated in a very long time, they may need some assistance in seeing the possibility for their own expanded growth. In this event, a visitation will occur in such a way as to allow them to see how narrow their view and ability to help others may have become. If this need should arise, they are often found listening to lectures, workshops and other growth processes around the world. Sadly, it is possible for us to become complacent and a bit out of touch. This process could assist in the ultimate growth of many very old souls. ("Old" in this context simply means that they have incarnated many times and have a great deal of growth behind them.)

At this level, one has the ability to maintain an image of one's choosing. In many cases, souls will look like someone they have been in a lifetime that was especially important for them. The sense of smell and taste has returned! While most will maintain an image, you will begin to see some that will move about in the essence of their energy with no particular form or shape. Sometimes when we see these souls draw near to Earth, we may see them as "orbs" of light. Remember that there are no physical bodies, only etheric ones.

Level Four: The Realm of Peace

The realm of peace contains the schools for teaching "Master Level Teachers," "Protectors" and "Spirit Guides." Here we find special schools for the re-education of the "Old Ones" and the "Wise Ones." Sometimes we feel there is nothing new to learn, and at that very moment, we discover just how much more there is to reconsider and relearn. When we refer to souls as being "old," that does not mean they were created at a different time, thereby making them older. The word "old" is used as a defining point for those who continue to incarnate and continue to grow. These are often some of the most gentle, most caring and loving of all souls. When one of these special ones crosses your path, more often than not you will be blessed by their very presence. You will feel the energy they carry and not understand why you feel so much better for having visited with them for a while. They do not seek or desire attention for the special gifts and abilities they have.

In some of the classes at this level, situations are created to mimic an actual physical existence. Those in this level of training will feel all the sensations of a truly physical body. They will feel pain, hunger, desire and every other feeling you and I feel today. If they pass the test, and this one is very difficult, they are allowed to become "Teachers" and "Great Advisors." This may be burdensome at times and requires the highest level of integrity and honor in the work they choose.

Between Level Four and Five, an extraordinary place of learning exists. This is known as a "Shanra." At one time, there were many of these schools, but today only one is in use. I am not sure why that is true or when it might change. Very few souls will study in this unique environment. It is a place where one will learn at every level the complete history of humanity.

There is no confusion on Level Four, only the most incredible peace, joy and beauty imaginable. There are many very good souls at this level. Some will enjoy peaceful and quiet lives and do not choose to reincarnate. They are allowed to make this choice because of the work they have done in the past. Even though this choice has been made, many continue to do extraordinary work throughout other levels, other dimensions and on Earth. There are so many souls working from various levels seeking self-fulfillment that the choice not to incarnate does not create a need or imbalance for others seeking help on their journey.

Level Five: The Realm of Sleep

This area is often referred to by many names. The souls who dwell here are brilliant and sensitive. These are the ones who travel to Earth and other dimensions performing miracles. These are the "Healers" and they are aware of all things – past, present and future. Many of the souls here will sleep and provide their energy to those who are working in the realms below. The souls here will make great sacrifices for the things they believe in. When I say, "what they believe in," this is not related to a religion or belief system that is associated with Earth itself. This is a belief in humanity and the ultimate preservation of the soul.

In "spirit" there is no difference except those that souls impose on themselves as part of their growth process. The soul, in its truest form, does not have any of the discriminatory differences that are present on Earth. In truth, we are all the same – we are all equal.

There are few words known to us that would describe the beauty of this place. Some souls will create islands for themselves; some will have magnificent homes and the most incredible music is everywhere. The experience of taste and smell is available but seldom utilized at this level. There is such a deeper understanding and connection with the Creator that most experience. The way the Creator is understood while in your physical body is pale in comparison to the joy of being one with the highest consciousness.

The love and peace felt in this realm is what we long for without understanding what pulls at us. Sometimes we experience a weariness, a longing for a place and feeling that we cannot describe and do not quite remember. When souls are at this level, it does not mean that they will not choose to go through the challenge of the lower levels again. Sometimes the more evolved the soul, the more often it moves through all of this again and again. Actually, there is great wisdom in making such a choice.

At this level, there is a great deal of communication between families. The term "families" used here is not necessarily the people you are related to now. While some of us do reincarnate within the same family cluster, the souls of our spirit family are the truest connection we know. This will help to explain why some of us feel connections to people we meet and feel an instant recognition. Do not loosely apply the over-used term "soul mates" to these connections. Truly, it is much more than that. Level Five is the largest of all the realms!

Level Six: The Realm of Creation

The love and peace felt at other levels pales in comparison to what exists here. It is more than just a feeling or experience; it becomes the existence that is one with the soul and all things. When you see the energy in this place, it compares a little to the Aurora Borealis. There is such an infusion of tone and color vibration that it is almost like looking at a mirage.

When you see a flower, for example, if you try to touch the petals you become part of the flower. The flower almost seems fluid as your hand passes through it. In "spirit," we do not have physical bodies, but from this level, you have the ability to attain the similarity of a body you have had before. You can project the image of a physical appearance or be in your more pure energy form.

All of the greatness, at this level, is just a thought away. Our thoughts have always become our reality, but in this place, it is expressed and created in its purest form. While great homes, buildings and churches can be found here, they are representative of a desire rather than a necessity. From this place, you do not require much of anything, but the experience of anything is available to you.

In comparison, Levels Six and Seven will be the smallest. Here, you will find the homes of many "Master Level Teachers." It is interesting that we find the place of rest for these Great Ones but seldom find them here. They have the choice of resting or contributing to humanity. Needless to say, most are out working. This is the refuge, the resting place of souls that are busy creating new possibilities for everyone that needs the help. You will find that religious icons from most belief systems spend time here.

From this place there is work being done in more than one dimension and at more than one level at a time. Perhaps you will understand the phrase "parallel dimensions and simultaneous time." That might seem like an interesting place to be and you may hope to arrive soon, but consider this . . . When you are doing work inter-dimensionally and at more than one level, it creates a greater challenge in that you increase your accountability many times over. You will create different parameters for each situation. Why would anyone want to set up so many different possibilities to fail or succeed?

It is true that within each unfolding lifetime is the possibility to fail, but it also means there are the same number of chances to do extraordinary things. From this level of growth, it is more likely that the soul will experience great achievements in all things they do.

Remember that this is the level of creation! From this place great discoveries are born. Music of the soul is created and sent down through the various levels in profusions of colorful energies – much like a rainbow. The long-awaited cure for dreaded diseases is formulated and sent down in expansive energy, reaching as many as can receive the information. These creations are sent out in such a way that any soul of any race, color, creed, origin or nationality could receive any portion of the information. This helps to explain how it is possible for people of many nations to be pursuing the discovery of the same thing but in different stages. The discovery is sent out to all that can receive it. Depending on our ability to receive and translate, we pursue the "dream" accordingly.

Level Seven: The Realm of Oneness

This is the place of "oneness" with the Creator – as we understand that term. From this level, we have the ability to see all things, hear all things and experience anything we choose. From this place, you will see the expansive galaxies; you will be aware of different time lines and many levels of inter-dimensional work. You will find very few homes or great facades; there is little use for the pretense of images that serve no purpose.

The souls of this place contribute most of their time and energy to all creation – even beyond the scope of Earth. Many will sleep for centuries, offering all that they are for the use of others. Most of the great and historical teachings and religions will come from this level. The difference in views is not meant to confuse, only to offer an opportunity for growth and understanding from an enormous viewpoint. The confusion associated with these teachings results from mankind's interpretation and explanation. The wisdom here is meant to be universal in scope. It is of little importance that we do not always agree; it is the manner in which we disagree that causes our problems.

History shows us that some of the great spiritual teachings have been changed, or interpreted differently, throughout time. The energy that is embraced as "Christ," "Buddha," "Mohammed," "Allah" and others comes from here. A soul here will have few limitations and an extraordinary accountability.

It is possible to achieve any level of spiritual growth or fall from any of these places. Because everything we are is about "choice," we make decisions, sometimes good and sometimes bad, and move through the various stages accordingly. This does not make it "right" or "wrong." It is only a statement of where we are at any given moment in our journey.

Again, I thank Judy for her narrative. To learn more about Judy Goodman and her work, please visit: www.judygoodman.com

Instrumental Trans-Communication and the Spiritual Planes

I would like to begin this section with a personal anecdote. In August 2007, I attended a seminar in Mount Shasta, California, organized by Michael and Raphaelle Tamura, featuring Michael, James Van Praagh and Erik Berglund. Michael Tamura has been clairvoyant from childhood and he has spent his life training other clairvoyants. James Van Praagh is a medium who communicates with deceased individuals and who helped create the US television series, *The Ghost Whisperer.* Erik Berglund is a healer and musician who plays the harp.

At this gathering, I met a physicist with a doctoral degree who works at a New York hospital supervising radiation treatment for cancer patients, who told me a story. He related that a close female friend of his died at a relatively young age. One day, after her death, the phone rang and he answered it. The voice on the line was the voice of his friend who had died. She told him that she was calling to let him know that she was alright and adjusting to her new life in the spiritual world. The conversation lasted several minutes. They both said goodbye and the call ended. The physicist told me he was sure that the telephone call came from his deceased friend.

This was the first time I heard a story in which an electronic device was utilized by a spirit being to communicate with a human being. In December 2007, I learned more about this phenomenon when I attended a lecture given by Mark Macy, co-author, with Dr. Pat Kubis, of *Conversations Beyond the Light: Communication with Departed Friends & Colleagues by Electronic Means.* In Mark's lecture, I learned of research that has been done in which spirit beings have used devices such as audiotapes, telephones and television sets to communicate with humans on the physical plane. This type of communication has been termed Instrumental Trans-Communication or ITC.

One of the early researchers in this field was a Swedish film producer named Friedrich Juergenson, who in 1959 captured spirit voices when he was taping bird sounds. As he was playing the tapes back, he was startled to hear the voice of his own mother, who said, "Friedrich, you are being watched. Friedel, my little Friedel, can you hear me?[1]

This started a research project for Juergenson who subsequently recorded thousands of voices and in 1964 published a book in Swedish entitled *Voices from the Universe,* followed by another entitled *Radio Contact with the Dead.* As a filmmaker, Juergenson did a documentary on Pope Paul VI and became friends with the Pontiff, who himself became interested in the spirit voices caught on tape. Pope Paul VI even initiated his own ITC research project at the Vatican.

In 1967, *Radio Contact with the Dead* was translated into German and Dr. Konstantine Raudive, a Latvian psychologist, read it and became interested in ITC. Raudive created his own methodologies utilizing laboratory conditions. In one of his recordings, he too heard the voice of his deceased mother in a transmission, who used her usual nickname for him, saying "Kostulit, this is your mother."[2]

Raudive postulated that spirits could manipulate the white noise of radio static, generated when a tuner was set between stations, to create voice transmissions that could be caught on tape. Raudive called this Electronic Voice Phenomena (EVP) and published a book about it entitled *Breakthrough: An Amazing Experiment in Electronic Communication with the Dead.*

Raudive's experiments were treated with skepticism by the scientific community and two audio engineering firms in England, Pye Records, Ltd. and Belling and Lee, Ltd., embarked on replicating these experiments under controlled conditions. Despite stringent controls, paranormal voices were detected in these experiments. In 1969, Raudive shared a First Prize Award from the Swiss Association for Parapsychology and the faint paranormal voices heard on tape have been called "Raudive voices" in his honor.

What is particularly interesting is that when ITC researchers themselves die and cross over to the other side, they have been successful in contacting their earthly cohorts. In these transmissions, they have provided information about the spiritual realms that is consistent with information provided above by Echo Bodine and Judy Goodman.

Friedrich Juergenson died in 1987. While alive, he developed a close friendship with Claude Thorlin, a fellow researcher in ITC phenomena. Juergenson was noted to be psychically gifted himself and on the day he died, it is reported that he sent a telepathic message to Thorlin indicating that during his funeral ceremony, he would try to manifest an image of himself on Thorlin's TV.

Indeed, during Juergenson's funeral, Thorlin photographed images of Juergenson's etheric or energy body on his television, which appear in *Conversations Beyond the Light* and, with the kind permission of Mark Macy, are also provided at the end of this chapter. In *Conversations Beyond the Light,* other images of deceased individuals are also provided, some of which were imprinted on the hard drives of computers. These additional images also demonstrate that we have a similar appearance in the spiritual world.

Let me describe a few other examples of ITC researchers who were able to contact their colleagues following death. George Meek, while alive, apparently received a telephone call from fellow researcher Konstantine Raudive after Raudive died in 1974. Jules and Maggy Harsch-Fischbach founded the Trans-Communication Study

Circle of Luxembourg (CETL), an organization dedicated to ITC research. On February 4, 1993, they found a text message on their computer from their departed colleague, Ernst Mackes, who died on November 26, 1992. On March 4, 1993, they found an image of Ernst on their computer, apparently transmitted from a spiritual plane. It showed Ernst looking like his old self, wearing the glasses he wore in life, sitting under a palm tree in a tropical scene in the spirit realms.

These ITC observations that we can maintain facial features in the spirit world consistent to those we had in physical life have also been affirmed by clairvoyants Echo Bodine and Judy Goodman. Michael Tamura, who consciously travels to and experiences the spiritual world while he sleeps, has often stated that we have the same appearance on the other side.

Spirit Photos

ITC observations give credence to the idea that we have an energy body that serves as a template for our physical body. Echo Bodine has provided another piece of evidence that supports that we have a spiritual energy body that resembles our physical body. Echo was given a set of photographs taken by a Minnesota police officer, who took the pictures just after a fatal automobile accident occurred. They show the face of a young man in spirit form that is a replica of the deceased young man in physical form, floating above the crash scene.

The young man appears to be caught shouting, "No!" expressing that he was not ready to die. The dynamic facial posture of the boy's spirit form contrasts with the boy's physical form, which is slumped forward, face down on the front seat inside the car. This dynamic facial posture argues against a double exposure or other mechanical camera failure. This photograph of the face of the young crash victim, hovering above the car in a spirit energy form, can be found at www.ReincarnationResearch.com under the "Spirit Communication and Ghost" category.

Nature of the Spirit World According to ITC Contacts

Numerous messages have been received from the other side by ITC researchers. I refer you to *Conversations Beyond the Light* for details on the sources of these messages. I will summarize some of their content below:

- Regarding the process of death, it is indicated that we remain in the vicinity of our body after we die and that we remain close to our loved ones, though the surviving will see the deceased person's energy body only if they are clairvoyant. Even if not clairvoyant, relatives may feel the presence of the deceased person. Individuals who have died can attend their own funerals and hear their eulogies. The feeling after death is one of lightness and freedom, as if a "heavy suit of armor"[3] has been shed.

- After shedding the physical body, we live in an etheric body, an energy body which underlies the physical body. The etheric body later disintegrates, which allows us to transition to the spiritual or astral planes where we have an astral body. In the transition to the astral plane, some may fall asleep and wake up in the astral planes not knowing how they got there. Others may remain conscious during the transition. Individuals may wake up in a hospital setting. Loved ones and pets who died previously may be waiting for the newly deceased person.

- In a hospital or other healing setting, the newly deceased adjust to life in the spiritual world. Those who had amputations receive guidance on how their astral limbs will regenerate through thought. People who died at an elderly age will become younger and those who died in childhood will grow older until a desired age is reached, usually appearing to be 25–30 years of age. When leaving the hospital, one finds surroundings similar to Earth, but more vibrant. Note that this ITC description of a hospital or healing setting is similar to the Pink Place that Echo Bodine described.

- ITC messages indicate that there are planes of existence in the spirit world that are similar to the levels described by Echo Bodine and Judy Goodman. The places that most humans travel to following death, as described in ITC communications, are the lower, middle and higher astral planes. The lower astral planes are similar to the lower planes that Echo describes: they attract people who are focused on survival, who are of lower levels of evolution. In his lecture, Mark Macy commented that these are the "dismal planes," similar to what we would imagine purgatory or hell to be like. It is described that petty thieves, pickpockets, adulterers, liars and fraudulent businessmen congregate here. Murderers are observed trying to kill each other, who become frustrated because nothing can be killed in the spiritual realms.

  It is described in ITC communications that communities can be locked in time and that people in Stone Age villages or ancient Viking settlements can thus perpetuate their existence. Reincarnation and further development can be delayed if the soul chooses. Recall that Ahtun Re made the same observation – evolution and reincarnation can be delayed by the soul, though not forever. When these souls do reincarnate, they aren't as developed as other souls, which accounts for the diversity in levels of evolution on the Earth plane.

  Ethical and evolved individuals go to the middle astral planes, which consist of beautiful landscapes, pleasant dwellings, cities, concert halls, schools and universities. People can be aggregated in communities based on religion, culture, ethnic group, race or other factors that one identifies with. Though this type of voluntary segregation occurs on the middle astral planes, a more universal outlook is gradually developed and indeed, must be attained, for entrance to the higher astral planes that reflect the concept of heaven.

  Creative individuals like artists, musicians, scientists and philosophers enjoy the astral worlds, as they can pursue their interests, including ITC research, much as they did on Earth but without the need to make a living. ITC researchers who have died describe a facility in the astral planes called Timestream, where they work on developing ways to contact ITC researchers on Earth through electronic means. Those who enjoy recreation, such as playing golf, can recreate their avocation as much as they like, though souls eventually get bored of things like playing golf and then seek further development. In the astral planes, synthetic food can be created, including meat, though no animals are killed to create food.

ITC messages indicate that higher planes exist, called the mental-causal planes, which are the source of technical and artistic breakthroughs. These are telepathically sent down to Earth to those who can receive the ideas. Judy Goodman, we recall, described this plane as "Level Six: The Realm of Creation."

Even higher planes, called the celestial planes, are known, which are closer to God. This is where Ascended Masters and great spiritual teachers reside. Those in the higher astral planes know of the celestial planes, though they have not experienced these highest levels of the spiritual world.

One can travel to specific planes based on the frequency that has been developed. In general, we are no different after we die. Those who are less evolved go to communities consisting of less evolved beings, while those who have worked on their spiritual evolution on Earth will congregate on higher planes.

- In the spirit world, memory of all past lives is restored and we may seek out friends from prior lifetimes.

- Friedrich Juergenson, in a computer contact that occurred in 1992, stated: "Beings keep their individuality during 'reality changes' with their consciousness and reincarnations."[4] Juergenson later reported from the astral plane in 1993 that "all thoughts are nothing but telepathy."[5]

- Friedrich Juergenson, from the astral plane, commented: "If you didn't solve your problems on Earth, they will be waiting for you here. In this new reality, the titles and positions that you held on Earth are unimportant. What remains is *your soul.* What is really important here is your ethical feelings and the humanities, all things of a constructive nature."[6]

• ITC communications indicate that individuals take their problems with them after they die. It is advised that Earth is the best place to work out problems. The astral world is described as a dream world, where you can theorize and plan to make evolutionary changes. On Earth, you are confronted with your actions and the consequences of those actions: it tests what you really believe in.[7]

• Based on ITC communications from the astral plane, Kubis and Macy came to the following conclusions. "The point is that one can create many mental constructs and play with ideas on the astral plane. But actually living on Earth is putting one's ideas into nitty-gritty practice. Life is the acid test of what one really believes in."[8]

• Individuals can space travel mentally to other dimensions or planets; can use dirigibles, hot air balloons or airplanes; surface travel by electric cars or motorcycles, depending on how they like to travel.[9]

Towards the end of *Conversations Beyond the Light,* it is pointed out that Thomas Edison, who invented the light bulb among many other things, made a serious attempt to create an electronic device that could be used to contact deceased souls. Mark Macy and Dr. Kubis end their book with instructions on how people can do ITC experiments themselves. To see ITC videos, hear ITC recordings and learn more about ITC, go to the web site: www.worlditc.org

Just as the radiation health physicist described at the beginning of this section, who I met at the gathering in Mount Shasta, never expected to get a phone call from his deceased friend, we may be surprised at what new ITC technology emerges in the future. To me, it is interesting that spirit messages obtained though electronic means seem to corroborate the experiences of Echo Bodine, Judy Goodman, Michael Tamura and Ahtun Re.

Conclusion

A common feature of these descriptions of the spiritual world is that there are gradations based on levels of consciousness. The more that we develop on Earth, through understanding ourselves and others, by expressing love to others, by developing the unique talents and energies that we are born with, by increasing our intuitive and psychic abilities through meditation, the closer we can get to God in the spiritual planes.

Judy describes that on the highest planes, we become aware of multiple dimensions and time lines, and that we can experience anything we desire. Echo relates that the highest planes represent retirement in the greatest sense. ITC research, a separate and independent source of information, provides a survey of the spiritual planes which is consistent with the experiences of Echo and Judy. Ahtun Re describes how he can merge with God, losing his individuality, then step his consciousness down to regain a separate sense of self. Ahtun Re describes his existence as being in "lucid ecstasy." This state of consciousness, this plane of existence, represents the fruit of our journey, of all our lifetimes on Earth.

In Life   In Spirit

Friedrich Juergenson discovered spirit voices recorded on tape while tap-ing bird songs. He become a pioneer in Instrumental Transcommunication (ITC). During his own funeral, he imprinted his image on the TV of his friend, Claude Thorlin. ITC images support the premise that an energy body maintains physical resemblance from one lifetime to another

10

Past-Life Reviews, Retention of Past Life Personalities, Holograms of the Soul, Ghosts and Multiple Universes Explained

It is commonly written in reincarnation literature and affirmed by Ahtun Re that after an individual dies, that person undergoes a review of the lifetime that has just ended. Not only do we view important life scenes as we remember them, but in addition, we are able to perceive these scenes from the perspective of others. We experience the joy or sorrow that we have caused in the hearts of others. Humorous portrayals of past-life reviews can be found in the movie *Defending Your Life* that features Albert Brooks and Meryl Streep.

Ahtun Re has indicated that in the spirit world, we can review all of our past lives, not just the most recent incarnation. Further, Ahtun Re has explained that one can even meet one's own past-life personas and have conversations with these personalities. This demonstrates that past-life personas are not lost once death occurs, but that these identities are retained within the soul.

An example of this personality retention is contained in a story that Kevin Ryerson related to me. At a public demonstration of channeling, one of Kevin's spirit guides, the Irishman Tom MacPherson, was answering a question from an audience member on the fabled civilization of Atlantis. Tom gave his answer in a simple, straight-forward way, but the audience member felt it was not sufficiently detailed.

Tom then told the man to hold on, that another entity was coming through to address the question. A different spirit guide then started to speak through Kevin, who lacked Tom's heavy Irish brogue, and who gave the questioner a more detailed explanation which he found satisfactory. Tom MacPherson then came back and asked if the audience member was happy with the answer. Tom then remarked that the entity who spoke was his own past-life persona, that is to say a past incarnation of Tom MacPherson himself in Atlantis.

As an interesting aside, in his book *Spirit Communication,* Kevin points out that when Tom MacPherson was incarnate and living in England in the era of William Shakespeare, Kevin himself was a magistrate in a court of law. MacPherson eked out his living, in part, as a pickpocket, and was occasionally brought for trial before Kevin. A relationship was forged in that era that has resulted in MacPherson serving as a spirit guide to Kevin in contemporary times. Kevin points out that people we have known in past incarnations will serve as spirit guides to us when they are not incarnate. Similarly, we who are now incarnate in physical form will one day serve as guides to our current spirit guides, after we have left the body and they reincarnate.

Ian Stevenson Xenoglossy Cases Support Retention of Personality within the Soul

Xenoglossy refers to the ability to speak and understand a foreign language that hasn't been learned by normal means. Xenoglossy represents strong evidence of reincarnation, as the ability to know the foreign language in these cases is thought to derive from a past lifetime in which the language was learned.

Several xenoglossy cases researched by Ian Stevenson, MD at the University of Virginia, dramatically demonstrate how past life personalities can indeed be retained intact within the soul. The most compelling example involves the reincarnation case of Sharada | Uttara

Huddar, which is featured with other xenoglossy cases in my book, *Born Again, Expanded International Edition*, as well as on:

www.ReincarnationResearch.com

Sharada, the past life persona, lived in nineteenth century Bengal. Her statements regarding her past incarnation, including specific names of family members, were objectively validated. Sharada could only speak Bengali, while the contemporary personality, Uttara, could only speak the Indian language of Marathi.

Sharada would take over Uttara's body for weeks at a time. Uttara had no memory of what happened during the Sharada phases and Sharada had no awareness of Uttara. Further, Sharada was not aware that she had died, even though she had no comprehension of twentieth century technology. She seemed to be a nineteenth century Bengali woman who was transported through time with her personality intact, emerging through Uttara's body. As such, what Ahtun Re described to me regarding past life personalities being retained intact within the soul is corroborated by this and other xenoglossy cases, which were meticulously researched by Ian Stevenson.

Grey Eagle, a Past Life Personality, Emerges through Kim Adams

Another example that demonstrates how past-life personas can be retained within the soul involves the case of Kim Adams, who publishes a community newspaper in Iowa. Kim became involved in investigating a past lifetime, as well as the phenomenon of mediumship, quite unexpectedly. He relates that he has had a lifelong habit of singing to himself when driving. One day in 2005, while going down the road and singing to himself, Kim noted that he was singing in a language he didn't understand. It sounded like a Native American Indian tongue, though he wasn't sure. Over time, Kim started to speak other languages which he also didn't understand.

I have invited Kim to narrate the turn of events which allowed him to gain more information regarding the xenoglossy that he was experiencing. In these passages, Kim refers to Dee Loecher, his beloved girlfriend.

> *One day, we were in Cedar Rapids, Iowa at a presentation by Canadian psychic Marilyn Rossner. Unknown to Dee, I approached Marilyn after her presentation, told her about the languages and asked her for advice. She said, "Next time the words come, take a pen and paper and see if you can translate them."*
>
> *Dee and I were driving home from Cedar Rapids when the words spontaneously started coming and since I was driving, I handed Dee a pen and a pad of paper. All of a sudden, she just started to understand. She wrote down her translations (we have about 400 pages of this now). That day, I spoke in several languages. All of them Dee could understand.*
>
> *Frequently, Dee will miss the first words of a "new" language coming through, then will be able to hone in on the frequency and the translations come readily to her. There have been only a couple times when she simply couldn't understand a language. The only foreign language I know is German, and I recognized that language during one session. We have heard words spoken in what sounds to us like Latin, French and Croatian, or some language similar to that.*
>
> *Often Dee (and sometimes I too) will see visions of what is going on when the languages are being spoken. Dee will say, "He's showing a picture of . . ." whatever. One day, while Dee and I were at a symphony concert, a language came through with a very excited energy – the person was a violin maker, and extremely enthused to be "hearing" a symphony again through my ears. He seemed to be speaking in Czechoslovakian, although neither Dee nor I knew for sure.*
>
> *One of the languages that came through on that first day was of an American Indian. We did not know until later that this person was "Grey Eagle," a Native American who appears to*

have lived in the mid-1800s in southern Oregon. He claims to be me, and claims that I am him. Grey Eagle is the primary contact we have with languages. He is always with me although he will step out of the way for others to speak as well.

Some languages don't even seem to have an Earthly base, and are extremely difficult to vocalize with this human body. This whole experience is very extraordinary, yet Dee and I simply seem to take it all in stride. We both feel strongly that these languages are important for our future and perhaps that of the planet. It is an important part of our spiritual path, so we go with it.

We have come across about eight other people who, after experiencing my languages, have started, or for the first time allowed themselves, to publicly speak in languages they don't know. Each time, Dee has been able to translate. We've even had two people, one in Iowa and one in Oregon, who've never met and yet speak the exact same language!

Dee has been described as having "all the gifts" which a medium can possess, so it doesn't surprise me that she can translate languages she doesn't know. She moves into the energy, or tunes into the vibration of the language, and it comes clearly through her. Grey Eagle claims her as his spouse during his mid-1850s lifetime in Oregon, and Dee has "seen" Grey Eagle from time to time, and remembered various events from that lifetime. He often "shows" Dee additional visual cues to help us understand what he is communicating to us.

As Grey Eagle seemed to be the primary spiritual entity who spoke through Kim, Dee and Kim tried to determine what Indian language was being spoken. After contacting various resources and Indian tribes, they were directed to John Newkirk, the current chief of the Latgawa tribe of southern Oregon. Mr. Newkirk was able to validate that Kim was speaking the language of the Latgawa tribe. They learned that the Latgawa once consisted of about 400 tribe members, though numbers have dwindled over time. Kim and Dee asked Mr. Newkirk to translate written passages of the Indian language that Kim spoke and Dee had transcribed. They found that Newkirk translated the passages exactly the same as Dee had translated them, though Dee, we have pointed out, has never learned the Latgawa language.

In sessions with Kevin Ryerson, Ahtun Re verified that Grey Eagle is a past incarnation of Kim Adams and that Dee was indeed Grey Eagle's wife, a Latgawa Indian named Shining Moon. I asked why Kim couldn't understand the Latgawa language while Dee could. Ahtun Re replied that for Kim, there is the issue of a memory block, whereas Dee has both an innate recollection of the Latgawa language and a psychic gift for understanding other languages she has not learned in her current incarnation.

The fascinating aspect of Kim and Dee's story is that it again demonstrates that past-life personalities live on in one's soul, as was also demonstrated in the Sharada | Uttara Huddar xenoglossy case and the anecdote involving Tom MacPherson and his past-life persona from Atlantis.

Holograms of the Soul

I asked Ahtun Re what the mechanism is that allows past-life personalities to continue to exist within the soul. Ahtun Re encouraged me to think of the soul as containing holograms or holographic memories of past lives, and that past-life personas can be recalled and projected as three-dimensional images. Kevin and his guides have referred to past lives as the childhood of the soul. Just as we can recall memories of childhood, the soul can retrieve and project past-life personalities. Imagine that you could project a holographic image of yourself as a child, an image that you could then interact with. This is what the soul can do.

The concept of the soul as an energy body that can project holograms can also be used to understand how split incarnation works. As discussed previously, split incarnation, also called parallel lives, occurs when one soul animates more than one body at one time. Imagine that the soul projects a hologram of itself, an energy template of itself, into more than one physical body simultaneously.

Each split emanates the same qualities or energies as that soul. After death, the experiences of each split are forever retained within the soul and can be recalled as holographic memories or images.

Using the hologram model, we can also understand the phenomenon of different people experiencing one person at different times and places. Ahtun Re has indicated that in the spirit world, we can meet and interact with any historical figure we are interested in, even if that person is incarnate on Earth. How can this work?

Let us use the example of Charlie Chaplin. The soul of Chaplin could project an interactive hologram of itself in the spiritual world, which could have conversations with other souls. At the same time, the soul of Charlie Chaplin could simultaneously project a hologram of itself on the Earth plane, animating a body. That is to say, the soul of Chaplin could be entertaining visitors in the spirit world while also having an incarnation on Earth and continuing its evolution on the physical plane. All of these manifestations truly represent the soul of Charlie Chapin, but in different forms.

Ghosts

Ghost phenomena can also be explained by holograms of the soul. Classic ghost stories involve a disembodied spirit haunting a house, often repeating the same activity over and over such as dragging chains across a floor, walking up steps, jumping off a bridge, riding a horse across the spot where the soul in a past incarnation was thrown, fell off and died, etc. We can conceive of such repetitive manifestations as obsessions or compulsions of the soul. Obsessions are repetitive, intrusive thoughts such as "Did I lock the door?" Compulsions are repetitive actions, like washing one's hands over and over again out of fear of getting some infection or disease.

If a soul has repetitive thoughts about a house that it misses or the manner in which a lifetime was ended, that soul can send a holographic projection of itself over and over, in a compulsive way, to the physical scene of its obsession. This holographic projection of the soul, a ghost, can be seen or heard by human beings who are sensitive enough to perceive it. Individuals who act as a "ghost-busters," such as Echo Bodine, serve as psychotherapists to these souls, helping to break the obsession.

Multiple Universes and Dimensions

The model of the soul being able to produce holograms can also be used to describe existences in multiple universes. Ahtun Re has indicated that in the five levels of the spiritual world beyond the seven levels that most human beings can perceive, other universes exist. In these other universes, Ahtun Re states that cities of light exist, including one called Shamballa.

Ahtun Re has revealed that spiritual beings who evolved on universes that predate our own, that existed before our Big Bang 14 billion years ago, live in these additional five levels of the spiritual world. An advanced soul, Ahtun Re has explained, can project a hologram of itself into a light city in one of these higher dimensions, yet also project itself onto the dense physical plane in a human incarnation. Indeed, many of the great spiritual masters of history are such advanced beings.

For most of us, the soul is much more complex and powerful than we can possibly conceive while our consciousness is locked into the physical plane in a human body. More and more information is coming out though, as in the cases of Kim Adams and Dee Loecher. I thank them for sharing their stories and thus contributing to an emerging science of spirit. As more such information is shared, through the Internet for example, a science of the soul will develop.

As previously noted, an organization called the Institute for the Integration of Science, Intuition and Spirit, has been founded to collect and analyze information about reincarnation, human evolution and the soul. It is hoped that with the collection of such information, human evolution will advance exponentially.

11

On the Nature of the Senses, Space, Time and Premonitions

On the physical plane, we experience time and are bound by time. In the spiritual world, according to Ahtun Re and many spiritual teachers, there is no sense of time, though there is the perception of space. Ahtun Re has described how he creates a holographic Egyptian temple where beings visit him, including clients of Kevin Ryerson. Ahtun Re has described that when beings enter his space, they emerge from a wall of light, are clothed in garb appropriate for them, and interact with him in the setting of his temple.

Tom MacPherson, another spirit guide who works through Kevin and who has a fondness for a lifetime in which he was an Irish pickpocket and part-time actor in Shakespeare's day, likes to recreate the setting of an Irish pub in his spiritual realm. In his pub, he meets people he counsels and interacts with. People are dressed appropriately for his pub, with some women even wearing the low-cut dresses that were fashionable during his lifetime in England. MacPherson says that in the spiritual world, a degree of physical reality can be created that is much like our reality on Earth.

I asked Ahtun Re about other senses like taste and smell, and more specifically, whether pizza is available on the spiritual planes. Ahtun Re noted that the senses can be recreated in the spiritual world based on memory, though it appears that a certain level of soul evolution must be attained to do so. If the soul can project a hologram of an Egyptian temple or an Irish pub, it stands to reason that a pizzeria could also be created.

Souls can also experience sensations vicariously through humans, though mediumship. Recall the story involving Echo Bodine's brother, in which a spirit guide played drums through her brother's hands. Kim Adams related that a deceased composer expressed great delight in hearing a symphony through his ears. Kevin has noted that beer was popular in ancient Egypt, and that Ahtun Re enjoys tasting our contemporary brews through Kevin's taste buds.

In the field of past-life regression therapy, it is hypothesized that spirit entities may become attached in unhealthy ways to people with addictions. For example, a soul who was addicted to alcohol in a past incarnation may attach itself to a human being alive today and psychically encourage alcohol abuse. So we see that mediumship can be used in beneficial ways, as a service to humanity as in the case of Kevin Ryerson, or in maladaptive ways, as in unhealthy attachments.

As noted, in the spiritual world there is no sense of time. Further, a soul can reflect on past incarnations at will, as if they were occurring in the present moment, much as we can watch and enjoy a favorite movie on DVD regardless of when that movie was made. The past life can be experienced as vividly as if it were occurring at the moment, just as a DVD replays a movie vividly over and over again.

On the physical plane, on the other hand, time does exist. One notion that has become popular in some spiritual circles is that all lifetimes, including future lifetimes, have already occurred and that all lifetimes occur simultaneously. Due to the popularity of these claims and the fact that this assertion makes no sense to me, I have asked Ahtun Re about this issue many, many times.

Ahtun Re has in turn indicated, many times, that the future has not already occurred and as such, future lifetimes have not already happened. Though the soul can reflect on past lifetimes that have already occurred on the timeline of the physical plane, the soul cannot experience lifetimes that have not yet occurred on that same timeline.

Ahtun Re explained that when people experience what they believe to be future lives, they are experiencing potentials for the future. It is entirely analogous to planning future events in the physical world, in your current incarnation, by creating a schedule. If you follow the plans you have made, you can predict where you will be in the future. That does not mean that the future has already occurred when you make the plans.

Just as one can plan a vacation that will occur six months from today, purchase tickets to fly to another continent and make hotel reservations in distant lands, in a similar way, a soul can plan out future lifetimes, visualizing the settings and the scenes. Indeed, numerous individuals in soul groups plan out incarnations together, with complicated itineraries and multiple points of rendezvous. However, planning a vacation or a lifetime is different from stating that either has already occurred.

One twist involves the ability of the soul to retain holograms of its past life personalities, personalities that can interact with you once you pass on to the spiritual world. For example, in a past-life review following death, if you interact with a past-life persona, that persona will perceive you as its future self. Still, this is a phenomenon that applies in the soul world: it does not violate the existence of a timeline on the physical plane.

Ahtun Re's affirmation that the future is still unformed is comforting to me, as it means that our lives, with the decisions and choices that we make, have meaning. We do create the future by our actions on the physical plane.

Premonitions

Though in general, we can consider that the future is unformed, premonitions can involve exceptions to this rule. Larry Dossey, MD has written a thought provoking book entitled *The Power of Premonitions*, in which documented cases of individuals apparently perceiving the future are compiled and presented. There are several ways in which premonitions can be explained.

Awareness of Future Plans

As discussed in the preceding paragraphs, an individual may become conscious of plans made by those in one's soul group. Ian Stevenson, MD of the University of Virginia conducted a study of 31 sets of twins whose past lives had been objectively validated. In every single case, which involves 62 individuals, the twins had significant past life relationships. The most common type of past life relationship was that of being siblings, followed by being friends & business associates, other relatives and spouses in their past incarnations.[1]

Past Life Relationships of Twins

Siblings 35 %
Friends 29 %
Other family relationships 19 %
Spouses 16%

Stevenson's twin study clearly demonstrates that souls can plan lifetimes in order to reincarnate with loved ones from past lives. If an individual on the Earth plane can perceive plans being made by a soul in the spirit world, then that individual can anticipate the future.

Indeed, this phenomenon is commonly observed in reincarnation cases, in that dreams predicting the upcoming incarnation are often experienced by future family members. Ian Stevenson observed this so frequently that he coined the term "announcing dreams" to describe this phenomenon, where a soul announces its upcoming incarnation to its future parents or other future family members. Announcing dreams are found in 22 percent of reincarnation cases researched by Dr. Stevenson.[2]

In my book *Born Again* and on the www.Reincarnation Research.com website under the categories *Planning Lifetimes and Relationships Renewed*, as well as *Spirit Beings in Reincarnation Cases*, examples of announcing dreams and souls planning their incarnations are provided.

Overviewing

Spirit beings can monitor events on Earth and can communicate events that are being planned through telepathy or via mediums. An example of overviewing occurred when I participated in a presentation with Shirley MacLaine in 2003, which took place in San Francisco. At that point, Shirley had already worked with Kevin Ryerson over a period of decades.

I was on stage with Shirley for almost two hours discussing reincarnation research. Though I was thoroughly enjoying myself, I was nervous about being on stage with such a famous celebrity. My anxiety was channeled into my right hand, which was holding a microphone. My hand grasped the microphone with greater and greater force until it started to cramp. At that point, perhaps forty minutes into our discussion, I passed the microphone to my left hand. After a while, my left hand started to cramp and I had to pass the microphone back to my right hand. This passing of the microphone baton continued throughout the duration of my stage appearance with Shirley.

What is remarkable about this incident with Shirley is that Kevin Ryerson's spirit guides were watching the proceedings from the spirit world. Kevin was in Portland during my event with Shirley, which, as noted, took place in San Francisco. Several months later, Kevin came to San Francisco to do a lecture and a public demonstration of channeling. In the session, a spirit guide channeled through Kevin, Tom MacPherson, came through. MacPherson is one of the primary spirit guides that Shirley has worked with.

Tom, through Kevin, addressed the audience in his Irish accent and called me out. Tom inquired, "So, Laddy, did you have a nice time with the redhead?" The redhead that Tom was referring to, of course, was Shirley MacLaine. I responded that I had a wonderful time on stage with Shirley.

Tom then noted: "You were a wee bit nervous, though, passing the microphone to and fro from one hand to another."

I was very surprised, even shocked, when Tom made that statement, as I had not told Kevin of the microphone incident. Later upon questioning, Kevin confirmed that he had no knowledge of my problem with the microphone when I was on stage with Shirley. This made me realize that Kevin's guides could monitor events on Earth, regardless of where Kevin himself was physically located.

Gary Schwartz, PhD, at the University of Arizona, has done formal overviewing experiments, in which spirit beings who communicate through mediums are asked to describe what subjects are doing at a particular time. The descriptions given by the spirit beings were then compared with logs created by the subjects themselves and scored by independent reviewers to determine the accuracy of the spirit beings' observations. Dr. Schwartz has reported positive findings, which are described in his book, *The Sacred Contract*.[3]

We can use the World Trade Center attacks as a theoretic example of how spirit beings could have used overviewing to help human beings on Earth predict future events. Once the suicide pilots were given their assignments, spirit beings could have been overviewing the planning of the attacks and thus have knowledge of which flights would be hijacked and what the respective targets were. These spirit beings could then have communicated the attack plans to human beings on the Earth plane via telepathic messages, dreams, intuitions or feelings.

Indeed, Dr. Dossey cites that the four jetliners that were used in the September 11 attacks had, in aggregate, an usually high vacancy rate of 79 percent. As the four planes were only 21 percent full, Dr. Dossey speculates that individuals somehow unconsciously knew to avoid these flights.[4] Spirit being overviewing is one mechanism in which telepathic warnings could have been issued.

Note that in this scenario, a premonition of the 9/11 attacks would have been based on knowledge of plans for the future, which if executed, would become the future. In this type of premonition, the future has not yet happened.

Let us use a case from Larry Dossey's book as another example of how spirit being overviewing could explain a premonition. In this incident, Dale Graff, a physicist and remote viewing researcher, dreamt that his wife's white station wagon had a small cylindrical object on the backseat, which began to glow bright red and then exploded, with fire enveloping the entire car. Dale checked the car but saw no leaks or other defects. Still, he took the car to a mechanic for a safety check, who found that insulation on wires attached to the fuel pump, which was inside the gasoline tank, were defective. As these wires further deteriorated, a gas tank explosion would have occurred.[5]

Ahtun Re has indicated that in this example, a mechanically inclined spirit being could have definitely surmised the situation with the car. Ahtun Re noted that spirit beings can detect conditions such as metal fatigue or in this case, insulation deterioration, through differences in energy patterns. This information then can be communicated to human beings through telepathic messages, dreams, intuitions or feelings.

Premonitions Not Explained by Planning of the Future or Overviewing

There are examples of premonitions which would be difficult to explain by the methods described above. Let us review two such examples from *The Power of Premonitions*.

Amanda's Dream regarding her Infant being Crushed by a Chandelier

Amanda, a mother living in Washington State, awoke at 2:30 AM from a nightmare, in which there was a violent rainstorm taking place. In the dream, a large chandelier that hung over her baby's crib in an adjacent room fell on top of the crib, crushing the baby. In the dream, Amanda stood in the baby's room surveying the catastrophe and saw that on a clock on a dresser read 4:35. She reported all these details of the dream to her husband, who dismissed the dream as silly.

Even though the weather was calm when Amanda awoke from her dream, she got up out of bed, went to the crib and took her baby back to her own bed. Approximately two hours later, Amanda was awakened by the chandelier crashing down onto her child's crib. She and her husband ran to the baby's room and realized that if Amanda had not moved her infant, the child would be dead. The couple observed that by this time, a violent storm had erupted and when they looked at the clock in the baby's room, the time was 4:35, the exact time that Amanda saw in her dream.[6]

Amanda's intervention could be explained by a spirit being perceiving metal fatigue affecting the bolt that held the chandelier to the ceiling, who then sent the dream to Amanda as a warning. It is difficult to imagine, though, that a spirit being could calculate the bolt failure so precisely in time, occurring at 4:35 AM.

Trolley Conductor Dream

Another extraordinary premonition Dr. Dossey cites in his book involves a conductor of a trolley car in Los Angeles. This conductor dreamt that as he was crossing a specific intersection in his southbound trolley, a northbound trolley, identified by the number 5, was approaching him. As he waved to the conductor in the northbound trolley number 5, a big red truck made an illegal turn and cut right in front of him, which resulted in a horrible crash. In the dream, three people were in the truck, two men and one woman, who were terribly injured in the accident. When he went to check on the woman, who had piercing blue eyes, she said, "You could've avoided this."[7] The conductor then awoke from the dream in a sweat.

Later on, as the conductor was doing his job, he found that the circumstances of his dream were replicated in reality. He was traveling southbound and was approaching the same intersection that he saw in his dream. A northbound trolley number 5 was approaching. He became nauseated at that moment and when the conductor from the approaching trolley began to wave, the conductor slammed on his brakes. Just then, a partially red truck drove into his path. If the conductor had not heeded his dream and did not apply his brakes, a collision would have occurred. The conductor then saw that there were three occupants in the truck, two men and a woman, who had piercing blue eyes. The woman with the striking blue eyes then signaled thanks to the conductor for preventing a crash.[8]

Dean Radin Premonition Experiments

In *The Power of Premonitions*, Dr. Dossey cites experiments designed and conducted by Dean Radin, PhD, the Chief Scientist at the Institute of Noetic Sciences (IONS), in which the central nervous system of subjects reacted to events before they happened.

In these studies, photographs, selected randomly by a computer, were shown to subjects. Sensors were employed to measure sweating of the skin and the size of pupils of the eyes of subjects. Stressful or dangerous situations trigger the body's "fight or flight" response, which causes increased sweating and pupillary dilation, that is, enlargement of the pupils.

In these experiments, it was observed that when the computer selected violent or sexual scenes, sweating and pupillary dilation of subjects increased several seconds prior to the image being shown. In contrast, when peaceful images were chosen by the computer, increased sweating and pupillary dilation were not observed prior to the image being displayed. As such, it appears that subjects somehow unconsciously knew when disturbing images would appear before the computer randomly selected these images. Further, the more shocking or disturbing the images were, the greater the measured presentiment effect.[9]

Dr. Dossey points out that 19 such studies have been done in different labs, 10 of which yielded statistically significant results, verifying that the autonomic nervous systems of subjects reacted to disturbing images before the images were randomly selected by a computer, while no such precognizant reaction occurred with the selection of peaceful images.[10]

Dr. Dossey also noted that in general, accurate premonitions are associated with events that involve large alterations in energy or entropy, such as explosions.[11] Further, most accurate premonitions involve negative events, such as disasters, as opposed to positive occurrences.[12] He also reported that accurate precognitive dreams are often "numinous," or more real than real.[13]

In a session with Kevin Ryerson, I asked Ahtun Re, the spirit guide channeled through Kevin who has demonstrated the ability to make accurate past life matches, about these types of precognition cases, where spirit being knowledge of future plans, or spirit being overviewing, cannot be used to explain the premonitions.

Monad-Mediated Premonitions

Ahtun Re related that these types of premonitions stem from involvement of the monad, which we have defined as the part of the soul that remains on the spiritual plane closest to God. The monad exists in a dimension that is not governed by the timeline experienced by those of us on Earth. The monad exists on a plane where time does not exist.

Ahtun Re explained that an individual's monad is continually gathering information through extrasensory means pertaining to its incarnations. Further, the monad is continually transmitting this information back to us, though we usually are unconscious of this process and unaware of the information being conveyed.

When a catastrophic event occurs, there is much greater energy in messages transmitted from the monad to the individual on the Earth plane. This is why dreams involving accurate premonitions often appear numinous and more real than real.

Events that threaten an individual's survival also increase a person's receptivity to messages from the monad. Just as we human beings filter out background noise in a busy restaurant so that we can engage in conversation, messages from the monad are often filtered out as background noise. When a message from the monad is related to the threat of one's survival, though, this type of message it is much more likely to get our conscious attention.

The key to understanding these types of premonitions involves the ability of the monad to transmit messages back in time, as perceived by human beings that exist in the Earth plane. Let us review this premise in the context of our premonition examples.

In the case of Amanda, Ahtun Re states that on the original timeline, the chandelier did fall and crush her infant at 4:35 in the morning. Amanda's monad observed this turn of events and sent an urgent, high energy message in the form of a dream, back in time, so that Amanda received this information at 2:30 in the morning, which prompted her to take her child from the crib back to her bed, thus saving the infant's life.

Amanda had free will in deciding whether to heed her premonition. By taking her child out of the crib, Amanda created a new timeline, a new sequence of events, and in doing so the original timeline, in which the infant was crushed, disappears. If Amanda did not transfer her infant from the crib, the original timeline would have been followed and would have been the ultimate reality in this story, in which her child would be dead.

Similarly, in the trolley car example, in the original timeline, the crash with the red truck, involving the woman with piercing blue eyes, did occur. The monad of the trolley car driver observed this accident and sent a powerful dream back in time to the conductor, along with the message that the accident could be prevented. The trolley car driver heeded his dream, prevented the accident and thus created a new timeline. As this happened, the original timeline disappeared.

In the Radin experiments, the subjects did see the images chosen at random by the computer and had emotional responses to disturbing images. This information was perceived by the monads of the subjects. The monads then telegraphed information regarding these disturbing images, which often dealt with violence or survival, back in time. In this way, the physiologic responses of increased sweating and pupillary dilation occurred, seemingly before the image was displayed on the timeline of the Earth plane.

Nobel Laureate Kary Mullis, PhD, who agreed to be featured as the reincarnation of Benjamin Rush in my book *Return of the Revolutionaries*, participated in a set of precognition experiments conducted by Dean Radin. Afterwards, Kary commented that the experience of knowing the future in advance was "spooky."[14]

Indeed, experiences that are based on messages from our monads, which function independent of time, are typically perceived as numinous, more real than real, and spooky.

Conclusion

In sum, we can conclude that in general, we create the future through our decisions and actions. The future is unformed. There is one timeline that we all experience in a consistent way.

There can be anomalies that we will term "monad-mediated premonitions," which are based on the monad observing events occurring along the timeline of the Earth plane and the transmission of information by the monad back in time to its incarnation on Earth. The monad's incarnation does have free will in regards to whether messages from the monad are heeded. If an individual takes action on the premonition, then the future can be changed and the original timeline disappears. As spooky as this seems, it does occur as evidenced by the cases and studies cited in *The Power of Premonitions*.

As such, let us visualize the timeline as a railroad track which has short spurs coming off of the main line. The spurs represent alternate timelines and realities that were short-lived, as information from the monad, transmitted back in time, resulted in a different reality which became integrated or synchronized with the main railroad line.

In this way we can understand how we do form the future with our actions, how the future is unformed, and still explain the phenomenon of premonitions. The timeline is like a train that is constantly moving forward. The monad can observe the progress of this train and when an obstacle is observed, the monad, which exists independent of time, can transmit information back in time to warn the train engineer of the obstacle.

Thought Travels Faster than Light

Ahtun has noted that thought travels faster than the speed of light. Further, information transmitted telepathically from the monad to an individual on the Earth plane is instantaneous. Though I do not fully understand it, Ahtun Re states that this property of thought, of traveling faster than the speed of light, is related to the monad's ability to transmit information back in time.

12

Child Prodigies: Picasso, Rubens, Beethoven and Michelangelo Reborn

One of the most appealing aspects of reincarnation is that it provides a very simple and logical explanation for the phenomenon of child prodigies. If we return to our model in which the soul is capable of projecting holograms of itself into physical matter, we can imagine how a soul that contains knowledge and talent from prior incarnations can project, can download, this talent into the body of a child.

Let us consider the example of Alexandra Nechita, who has been identified in *Born Again* as the reincarnation of Pablo Picasso. Alexandra, starting as a toddler, was obsessed with creating artwork, though she received no direction from her parents or the environment to do art. In fact, her parents were concerned that Alexandra showed little interest in playing with other children or doing other things that children normally do. At age four, she started to draw figures with two faces and four eyes in Picasso-like representations of people. Picasso helped invent cubism and by the age of eight, having mastered cubism, Alexandra was known as the "Petite Picasso." She works in multiple media, creating even giant, Picasso-like sculptures.

Another child prodigy, artist Akaine Kramarik, spontaneously developed the ability to paint at the age of four after having an experience in which she states that she was taken to heaven. Her description of the experience is similar to that of Echo Bodine. Born into an atheist family in 1994, Akaine is self-taught in art and has related that "God is my teacher." Her visions have brought spirituality to her family and her paintings sell for $50,000 to $1,000,000. Akaine also writes poetry. As described on her web site, when asked where she learned to write, Akaine responded that it seems that ideas "have been planted in me." She has also written, "Through the Spirit, I experience other different lives." Again, imagine the model of Akaine's soul projecting a hologram of itself, downloading information into young Akaine's mind.

Though I am not clairvoyant, I do at times get accurate past-life information through intuitions. I always check such information with Ahtun Re, the spirit guide channeled through Kevin Ryerson, who has demonstrated an ability to make accurate past-life matches. When I first saw the colors in Akaine's art, which is often religious in nature, I immediately experienced an internal message that she is the reincarnation of Peter Paul Rubens, a Flemish Baroque painter who was born in 1577. I then noted that a self-portrait by Akaine bears a strong resemblance to one done by Rubens. Even the angle at which the head is held in both self-portraits is similar.

In a session with Kevin Ryerson, Ahtun Re agreed that Akaine is the reincarnation of Rubens. As Akaine is so young, I sought permission from her family to make this proposed past-life match public. I am grateful to Akaine's mother, Forelli Kramarik, for giving permission, which she did stating that I should have the freedom to express my ideas. It must be noted, though, that the assertion that Akaine is the reincarnation of Rubens is mine, not Akaine's nor her family's. To learn more about Akaine, go to: www. artakiane.com

Another child prodigy case involves Barbro Karlen, who has had memories since childhood of being Holocaust victim Anne Frank. The Anne Frank | Barbro Karlen case is presented in *Born Again*. Barbro demonstrated a gift for writing as a child, and at the age of twelve, she had a book of poetry and prose published. It was entitled *Man on Earth* and it became the best-selling poetry book in Swedish history.

Barbro appeared on television programs with ministers who were amazed that a teenage girl could speak so intelligently on matters like the soul, the nature of man, and the question of good and evil. Anne Frank demonstrated a similar talent and indeed, the reason that she became a symbol of the Holocaust is that her diary was so well written and addressed universal themes, such as the nature of humanity and whether man is good or evil. Like with Barbro, readers marveled at how Anne, as a young girl, could write so maturely on moral themes.

Even when talents are expressed later in life, we have observed how patterns from the soul are replicated in physical incarnations. One example involves the reincarnation of the artist Paul Gauguin, which is featured in *Born Again.* As a young man, artist Peter Teekamp, the reincarnation of Gauguin, unconsciously reproduced sketches that Gauguin created in adulthood. In the Laurel & Hardy | Bacher Boys reincarnation cases, also presented in *Born Again,* Josh and Danny Bacher instinctively resonated to Laurel and Hardy as children. As young men, they recreated the comedic development of Stan and Ollie by creating their own silent movie. In the reincarnation case of Dorothy Dandridge | Halle Berry, found in *Return of the Revolutionaries* and *Born Again,* the acting career of Dorothy Dandridge was continued in the persona of Halle Berry, and culminated in the winning of an Oscar.

Beethoven's Reprise

A musical child prodigy case involves the reincarnation of Ludwig van Beethoven. Recall that in the cases of Daniel Jurdi and Suzanne Ghanem, researched by Ian Stevenson, MD and cited in *Born Again* and *Return of the Revolutionaries,* it was demonstrated that individuals can reincarnate very quickly, even within a year of death. If it is a general principle that most souls reincarnate quickly and frequently, which I believe is true, this implies that famous individuals in history have been reincarnating all along. Though they have had additional lifetimes, we have not been identifying them in their subsequent incarnations.

As Beethoven was born in 1770 and died in 1827, we would expect that Beethoven would have had several incarnations between then and now. Indeed, I thought it probable that Beethoven is incarnate in contemporary times and I have been wondering who he might be. On February 17, 2008, I was watching a US television program entitled *Sixty Minutes,* which featured a segment on a young conductor from Venezuela named Gustavo Adolfo Dudamel, who is considered a musical sensation. In fact, the title of the television segment was "Gustavo the Great."

As I gazed upon his face, his hair and the passionate manner of his conducting, within moments I declared, "It's Beethoven." Seconds later, the program's reporter noted that the music Gustavo was conducting, with his hair bouncing wildly, was written by Beethoven. In a subsequent session with Kevin Ryerson, which occurred only six days after the television program aired, I was delighted when Ahtun Re confirmed that Gustavo Dudamel is indeed the reincarnation of Ludvig van Beethoven.

Gustavo was born on January 26, 1981. When interviewed on the *Sixty Minutes* program he related that he has been conducting ever since he was six years old. He started studying music as a child, took violin lessons and began formally studying conducting in 1995, at the age of 14. In years that followed, he won conducting competitions and by the age of 27, he became the principal conductor of Sweden's Gothenburg Symphony. In 2009, he became the musical director of the Los Angeles Philharmonic, becoming the orchestra's youngest director in its history.

In 2006, Gustavo married Eloisa Maturen, a ballet dancer, journalist and his long-term sweetheart. I inquired about past life connections between Gustavo and Eloisa, and Ahtun Re confirmed that Eloisa is the reincarnation of one of Beethoven's loves, Josephine von Brunswick. In one portrait of Josephine, a striking resemblance exists between her and Eloisa. Beethoven's romantic life was unrequited and he never married. In contrast, in contemporary times, the union between Eloisa and Gustave appears to be marked by joy.

Another tragic aspect to Beethoven's life is that he became deaf. At about the age of 26 he developed tinnitus, a medical term for ringing in the ears, which interfered with his hearing. By the age of 44, Beethoven was completely deaf, a condition he endured until his death at age 57. Despite his hearing impairment, Beethoven continued to compose some of the most beautiful music the world has known.

In a famous story which illustrates his poignant situation, when he first publicly conducted his Ninth Symphony, which contains the stirring piece, *Ode to Joy,* Beethoven only heard silence at the end of the performance. He was then turned to face the audience, which was applauding wildly. Taking in this sight, yet hearing nothing, Beethoven started to cry. In contemporary times, Beethoven has his hearing, as well as an immortal love. May "Gustavo the Great" and Eloisa have happy and fulfilling lives.

Michelangelo

At this point, I would like to present information regarding the reincarnation of Michelangelo. The way this case came to light is of interest. It started with an experience that I had in September 2006 in Florence, Italy. My wife Svetka and I went on a Mediterranean cruise and as part of a tour of Florence, our group went to see Michelangelo's David. As we were waiting outside the museum, we spotted a street vendor wearing a T-shirt with a "Union 76" logo.

Svetka and I couldn't believe it, as I had worked for this oil company, Union 76, also known as Unocal 76, as a medical director for 11 years. In my book *Return of the Revolutionaries,* I discuss the importance of the 76 symbol in my life as it relates to a past incarnation I had during the American Revolution, which was launched in 1776. Union 76 was a California-based company with operations in Indonesia. Even in the United States, I hadn't seen a Union 76 T-shirt since I left the company in 1997. How did this T-shirt wind up in Florence?

This unusual synchronicity made me wonder if Michelangelo had reincarnated in contemporary times. When we returned from our vacation, in a session with Kevin Ryerson, I asked Ahtun Re whether Michelangelo is incarnate. Ahtun Re told me that he is and that Michelangelo was living in Las Vegas. Ahtun Re added that he has been involved in designing movie sets and that he has created sculptures for casinos in Las Vegas. Ahtun Re declined to give me Michelangelo's name, stating that I should have no problem finding him.

I did an Internet search on artists and designers in Las Vegas and quickly was drawn to a model of an eighty foot tall sculpture of two giant boxing gloves striking each other, oriented in the vertical dimension. I thought to myself that this is something that Michelangelo would do, perhaps due to the scale, but there was also another reason, which I still was not conscious of. There was a phone number displayed with the boxing glove image and I called. A man answered and I related that I was trying to locate the artist doing the boxing glove sculpture. The voice replied, "That's me."

Paul-Felix Montez was the voice on the other end of the phone line and he stated that he had set up the phone number as a business line, which he rarely answered directly. I then explained the reincarnation research that I was doing, the work that I had done with Kevin Ryerson, and the fact that I was looking for the reincarnation of Michelangelo in Las Vegas. I continued that I was entertaining the possibility that he might be the one, but if he wasn't, I asked that he help me find the reincarnated Michelangelo, as he must know the artist community there. Paul then chuckled and said, "This is very interesting, as I have been in Las Vegas only a little over a year, yet three different people have called me the 'Michelangelo of Las Vegas.'"

Later on, Paul sent me photos of himself and I found that his facial features, including his unique, broad nose, were consistent with those of Michelangelo. In a subsequent session with Kevin, Ahtun Re confirmed that Paul-Felix Montez is a reincarnation of Michelangelo, though he also said that a split exists. I asked why

Michelangelo would settle in Las Vegas and Ahtun Re told me that in his Italian lifetime, his primary employer was the Roman Catholic Church, which limited the scope of work that Michelangelo could do. Las Vegas represents the opposite pole, where he has complete freedom to create what he wants.

I subsequently recommended that Paul study the life of Michelangelo, which he did. Finding many correlations, Paul soon put up his own web page about the correspondences between Michelangelo and himself, which he states that he found to be "astounding." Paul has been gracious enough to allow me to use his analysis in this chapter. Let me share some of his observations with you.

Childhood and the Demonstration of Talent

Michelangelo was raised in Florence and later, during the prolonged illness and after the death of his mother, he lived with a stonecutter and his wife and family in the town of Settignano, where his father owned a marble quarry and a small farm. I personally was orphaned when I was one year old, left by my father in the New York foundling home in Manhattan. The few papers recording my adoption there stated that my natural birth mother abandoned both father and child and that my birth father could no longer care for me. I was then adopted at two years of age into a New York Italian family.

Michelangelo started training in a crafts guild at an early age. Michelangelo early on impresses people with his ability to draw. He competes for a rejected piece of massive marble and is recognized for his creations in stone. In first grade, I do a drawing of a log cabin and teachers are amazed at my level of fine detail in drawing birds, tree bark, detail upon detail.

A book on anatomy was given to me by my grandfather, all written in Italian. I drew from it at age 7 or 8, even though it included nudes. Many studies by Michelangelo and da Vinci were in the book. In the third grade, I was chosen to paint a mural, "Arrival of Christopher Columbus," for a hallway 4 feet by 6 feet. In junior high school, I excelled in art, and became a special science student for one-on-one science explorations. At 14 years of age, I was chosen to paint a mural 26 feet long by 8 feet high for a school hallway, depicting various scientific achievements in the United States. Later, I was accepted into a specialized commercial art high school in Manhattan, New York.

Lacking money to go to college, I had few choices until a guidance counselor offered me an application to the Cooper Union School of Art and Architecture. Considering this is a free school, with an intense barrage of tests, portfolio submissions and reviews, I felt it was all I could do or hope for, and little hope for it was what I had. All I could do was "try." This college has 10,000 applications a year, and only selects 60 day-school students and 50 night-school students for each area in the school: art, architecture and physics.

The odds were a million to one, but somehow, during the exams, because I felt I had nothing to lose, I remember my mind saying, "Draw everything as you see it, feel it. Let it all go, the way you know inside. It is your own creativity and creations." After all, we were asked to draw the great old hall we were in, and so many were doing utterly realistic, shaded representations. I saw it as a "sculpture," dark strong lines, massive forms colliding into each other, around each other, and I drew it that way. And so I entered the Cooper Union School of Art and Architecture in New York City.

On Sculpture

Yes, I am a sculptor. Being a sculptor and a master of sculpture for over 30 years, I have done the large horses and statues found in Caesar's Palace in Las Vegas, figures for casinos, figures and sets for films such as Men in Black *and* Bat Man. *I was a member of the exclusive 55-members-only sculptors' ITASE local in the Film and Museum Exhibits architectural union. Today I am creating large-scale monuments for Las Vegas, and even proposing one of my own called* The Greatest.

When I asked Paul if he could do a sculpture such as Michelangelo's *David*, he responded:

> *Yes, without a doubt. I have done many big sculptures in classical anatomy – I am very good at it. I have a "great eye" for mass and line in sculpture; my peers have always said that. It's intuitive, even at distances. To the inch, I have always been able to measure by eye.*
>
> *I recently exhibited in a major one-man exhibit at the Las Vegas Art Museum, so my work has been validated by the arts community. Even now, I am joining forces with the city, the mayor, major real estate developers and the arts council to make large architectural projects happen.*
>
> *I appeared on the Discovery Channel TV series* Monster House. *In the show, working in 104-degree summer heat, I completed the carving of a two-storey, concrete-coated statue of the Egyptian Pharaoh Ramses. The producers' statement about this was that "no one has come on the show, worked so exactingly and fast, or ever truly delivered or done any such project so fast and with true integrity." It was a great compliment to my drive, training and skills. I have been a special sculptural live-action effects designer on such major films as* Batman, Congo, Indian in the Cupboard, Men in Black, Godzilla (*the remake*), Showgirls, Species *and many more. I have also designed sets, theme parks, theme stores, casinos, decorations, etc.*
>
> *Scope of Michelangelo's scale: Without a doubt, Michelangelo is renowned for creating some of the world's most iconographic, largest-scale art works, the most dynamic ever. For the Sistine Chapel,* David, la Pieta, *etc., he was considered the greatest sculptor of his time. I too make "Big Art." The reason I use that phrase is the dumbing down of our culture. The word "monumental" seems impossible for anyone to remember and sculpture has a semi-silent "p." So of necessity, humor, brand identity and fun, I say "Big Art."*

Michelangelo's David *is one of the world's most icono-graphic art images. I only recently saw it again, after working on my sculpture,* The Gloves, *the monument part of my two-part art work called* The Greatest, *a year before all this. The Gloves stands 80 feet tall in the model, is cast in stainless steel and bronze, and is fully engineered and ready for manufacture and installation once funding comes in.*

Michelangelo, who was often arrogant with others and con-stantly dissatisfied with himself, saw art as originating from inner inspiration and from culture. My view is similar: inner vision, something within, points me into a creative direction, haunts me, and I must create it. But as I create, it all of a sud-den takes on another dimension: why is this, what is it, how does it live in, reflect, exist with the cultural world around it? The iconography is a major concern plus the impact that it has on the viewer.

Michelangelo quote: "The greater danger for most of us lies not in setting our aim too high and falling short, but in setting our aim too low and achieving our mark."

When recently discussing my monumental sculpture and memorial to boxing, someone commented, "It takes in size, icon-ographic scale and visual identity, and goes one step further – time, and the simple promise of the eternal. It's big, in any and every sense one can apply to it."

On Writing and Poetry

Michelangelo was also a poet and writer. The sample below he wrote at age 57:

> "I feel as lit by fire a cold countenance
> That burns me from afar and keeps itself ice-chill;
> Λ strength I feel two shapely arms to fill
> Which without motion moves every balance."

I have written and had plays produced, sold TV shows, and writ-ten and won awards for screenwriting. The beauty of human interaction and motivation in such pared-down forms is awesome. One of my award-winning screenplays, called Bodega, *can be found on the New York City Film Commission's site in the category "Best Un-produced Screenplay About NYC."*

On Time

It is often quoted by Michelangelo that what he hated most in people was a time-waster. I find that this is true. Time is the only thing that can be lost and never regained.

On Sexuality

Michelangelo has been declared a homosexual by some. Though no specific evidence of this lifestyle is present, in his work David *there is an undeniable homo-erotic sensuality and power. Letters have also been found, attesting to his possible intimacies with young male models as lovers in his later years. Michelangelo was also a poet, and many of his poems contain references to adoration of the male form. This kind of sexual relationship was and still is common between older men and young men in Europe, as a rite of passage into sexual awareness and sexuality.*

Fundamental to Michelangelo's art is his love of male beauty, which attracted him both aesthetically and emotionally. In part, this was an expression of the Renaissance idealization of masculinity. But in Michelangelo's art, there is clearly a sensual response to this aesthetic. Such feelings caused him great anguish, and he expressed the struggle between Platonic ideals and carnal desire in his sculpture, drawing and poetry too, for among his other accomplishments, Michelangelo was also a great Italian lyric poet of the 16th century.

The sculptor's expressions of love have been characterized as both Neo-Platonic and openly homo-erotic; recent scholarship seeks an interpretation which respects both readings, yet is wary of drawing absolute conclusions. One example of the conundrum is the story of sixteen-year-old Cecchino dei Bracci, whose death, only a year after their meeting in 1543, inspired the writing of 48 funeral epigrams, which, by some accounts, allude to a relationship that was not only romantic but physical as well.

In contrast, in Michelangelo's later years, spanning some twenty years before his death, his writings all turn to one woman, and hers to him. Late in life, he nurtured a great love for the poet and noble widow Vittoria Colonna, whom he met in Rome in 1536 or 1538 and who was in her late forties at the time. They wrote sonnets for each other and were in regular contact until she died, though many scholars note the intellectualized or spiritual quality of this passion.

It is impossible to know for certain whether Michelangelo had physical relationships. If he did, he was likely bisexual, rather than a true homosexual, but different camps claim different things. In my opinion, it is much clearer and simpler. The depth of human passions, desires and needs, when unleashed in creativity as powerful as his, knows no bounds to their expression and fulfillment.

I would have to say about my own sexuality that I am bi-heterosexual. All of my long-term relationships have been with women, but I have explored the sexuality, even gender reality, of being with men. It is sexual openness that clearly for me led me to see the depth of emotional bonding with women, and the level of commitment that could ensue because of the honesty to reveal this depth of my soul, and thus they become deep soul-bonded relationships. For in this area, it is as if I am sharing the most vulnerable part of my being. It is a harder road to bare such honesty, but with much greater rewards. I feel it is destructive to believe that one's sexuality should be a secret from those one loves. How is that possible, to live a lie and never to rise to the real challenge of courageous relating?

But to live one's life in fear and deny that which is part of the search for meaning and truth is to deny spirituality its greatest importance: that we are all divine contributors to each other's existence. If we open up and deeply listen to each other, what an abundance of wisdom we possess. My struggles extend to a very narcissistic stepmother, a woman unable to bear children, surrounded by sisters who all had twins. What a strange turn of events, and how sad for her, but often this narcissism would be expressed, whenever I did something which displeased her, like an ailment: "I could have adopted two children, a boy and a girl, but at the time we only had one room and we adopted you. I saw them, though, before you, and a girl would have been my friend."

It took me many years to unravel the pain of this statement, the fear and abusive nature of it, but also unravel and come to see and love the depth of my stepmother's desire to be a woman, to give her love and how she missed out on realizing the depth of love I offered her as a "son," even though adopted, and that natural childbirth does not define a parent, love does.

So with this gender, emotional pain, deep desire to belong, be safe, be that girl for my family, and my father's rejection of my artistry as a homosexual pursuit – a conflict for him with my gifts, I could only begin a journey in New York City, Greenwich Village, in the gay community, which enjoyed my art and sculpture, listened, and applauded my work and young body.

On Eroticism in Art

Censorship always followed Michelangelo, once described as inventor delle porcherie *("inventor of obscenities"). The infamous "fig-leaf campaign" of the Counter-Reformation, aiming to cover all representation of human genitals in paintings and sculpture, started with Michelangelo's works. To give two examples, the bronze (actually, marble) statue of* Cristo della Minerva *(church of Santa Maria sopra Minerva, Rome) was covered by a pan, as it remains today, and the statue of the naked child Jesus in* Madonna of Bruges *(The Church of Our Lady in Bruges, Belgium) remained covered for several decades.*

I have exhibited my art works worldwide, and am in many museum collections. I have also created erotic art that is in erotic art museums worldwide.

On Physical Resemblance

One test is visual likeness. Here the intensity of the eyes, the same color, cheek bone structure, and most clearly the wide nose, all show the same physical traits.

On Spirituality and Creativity

Michelangelo's spirituality: It is often cited in biographies that he was very spiritual, and ethically so. In his lifetime, he was also often called Il Divino *("the Divine One"), an appropriate sobriquet given his intense spirituality. Michelangelo defended his privacy above all. When an employee of his friend Niccolo Quaratesi offered his son as apprentice suggesting that he would be good even in bed, Michelangelo refused indignantly, suggesting that Quaratesi fire the man. Moral integrity.*

But the greatest thing I experience everyday is the work that I love and, most importantly, burning, raging creative visions of new art works, new possibilities, new meanings to explore in art. I have art representatives in both NYC and LA. I have gained the support of real estate developers in Las Vegas for my large-scale sculptures and public works. They see the project and are excited by it and what it offers for the new 21st century city of Las Vegas, no longer the small town. Each day I wake up excited and work ten, twelve hours on art and art-related business, or designing for various theme designs, set design projects. Then in the evenings, I watch the evening sky, the stars, the world of nature. A quiet walk, and I work out with weights so I can be as physical with my work as possible, tingling throughout my body as a receptor of all and everyone around me.

The grandeur of the visible and invisible universes entwined about us – what a daily awareness and vast show to see and be part of, to act and create from! It is all such a meditation on existence and its glorious abundance, and then there is love and sex, laughter, friends and simple joys. We all have it all, if only we weren't so blinded and could stop and see, listen, feel with the wisdom of the ages, the fearless freedom of Dante's great statement, "Wear death on your shoulder, be not afraid of it, for time is your greatest enemy, for there is so little of it."

Very close friends have often stated that I am very spiritual. To have such faith in my visions seems to demand so much more than myself. A past life perhaps? One of my favorite spiritual questions to ask is: "What is your vision of your life when you are seventy-five years old? Is it filled with inspiration?" With a true friend of mine, I asked that question ten years ago in Los Angeles. He said he didn't know.

I answered, "I see myself building large-scale sculptures in the desert: big, and with many people, all of us joyously inspired." Today, Las Vegas Big Art and The Greatest *are exactly that. I emailed this friend when I had finished the models and said, "Look at this, the vision we talked about," and he said, "Now we have to make it to 75," and we will.*

I have also found those who suffer, carry great baggage or have deep troubles cannot contemplate this question regarding vision, even for one second. It is as if they have given up hope, wallowing in the self-pity of the past and even their own present, which they see as doomed. May you envision in your life to inspire, for only that vision is true.

I hope you can see, as I have, how so many things are similar between us, between Michelangelo and me. In reincarnation there is value, substance, spiritual confirmation of who and what we are doing, seeking and envisioning in our daily lives.

The similarities can be coincidence, but now that I am looking at them, I wonder, for so many symbolic gestures took place – incidents in my life, in school, choices that I made but never made, as a destiny was being played out, and many burning, intense, passionate desires being created endlessly. Could all this be my doing? It never felt that way, as if I were the sole

*director of my life. Inspirations, visions to live, goals and de-
sires melding into what I now look back on, and even see as my
future, seem to be entwined into this other life, this past life, of
another sculptor called Michelangelo.*

In conclusion, recall that the first piece of art that I saw created by
Paul-Felix Montez was his sculpture, *The Gloves,* which, in fulfillment, will be an 80-foot-tall sculpture consisting of two boxing
gloves, one striking the another. At that time, I had the thought that
Michelangelo might do a work such as this, consciously thinking of
the size of project, remembering that *David* was nicknamed, "the
Giant."

It wasn't until after Paul wrote his article on the correspondences between Michelangelo and himself that I realized another
significant parallel. Paul compared a scene from the Sistine Chapel,
where the finger of God touches the finger of Adam, with his sculpture. I then realized that when I viewed *The Gloves,* I was unconsciously reminded, in its 21st century Las Vegas version, of God's
finger giving life to Adam.

I am not an art historian, but I have read a little about Michelangelo. In my perception, it seems that in the paragraphs featured
above, we hear the voice of the sculptor from Florence who lived
500 years ago.

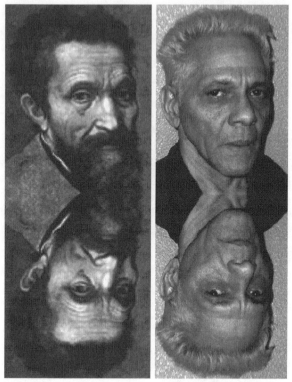

Michelangelo   Paul-Felix Montez

Portrait of Michelangelo courtesy of The Metropolitian Museum of Art, Gift of Clarence Dillon, 1977(1977.384.1) Image © The Metropolitan Museum of Art

**Paul-Felix
Montez**

Michelangelo
Courtesy of Teylers Museum, Haarlem

**Paul-Felix
Montez**

13

Bodhisattvas and the End of Reincarnation

I asked Ahtun Re what determines when the cycle of incarnation will end for an individual. As a being who has not incarnated in over 3,000 years, I thought that he should know. Ahtun Re's answer was quite simple. He stated that reincarnation is no longer mandatory when an individual has:

- developed his or her own unique talents and abilities to a level of competence
- demonstrated these abilities with joy
- worked off or neutralized karma incurred on the physical plane, which can be accomplished by experiencing what one has done to others or through service
- developed an inclusive love for all of humanity

I asked Ahtun Re how many lifetimes are required for people to attain this liberation. Ahtun Re told me that 80–120 lifetimes of experience are necessary for most souls.

I then asked Ahtun Re a series of questions regarding bodhisattvas. I use this term simply to describe individuals who reincarnate not out of necessity, but voluntarily, out of the desire to help humanity grow and evolve. I know that various Buddhist philosophies use the term "bodhisattva" to denote a certain level of enlightenment or spiritual achievement. I use it to mean individuals who volunteer to incarnate on the physical plane out of a sense of service, even though they are not obligated to do so to redeem karma or to live lessons that have to be learned. A bodhisattva in this context is a person who has completed cycles of incarnation on Earth and has the option to stay in the spirit world, in heaven, but who elects to reincarnate again out of compassion for humanity, to help other human beings evolve.

I have always thought that the number of bodhisattvas on planet Earth must be very small at any given time. I was surprised when Ahtun Re told me that he estimated that 20 to 30 percent of the Earth's population has developed to the point where these individuals did not have to return to Earthly incarnation, but did so as a service to humanity. This implies that one does not have to be a saint to have completed the cycle of reincarnation, that many commonplace, good people have achieved bodhisattva status.

I found it reassuring to know that this high level of development is not so far out of reach. It also made me reflect that if more of us knew that we have reincarnated voluntarily, life might be a little sweeter. Due to the demands of the world, it may be difficult to imagine that we chose the lifetime that we are in. But if we know that we did so choose, to help the ones we love or humanity as a whole, this knowledge provides a greater purpose to life and may help us appreciate the little wonders that surround us on this, our planet, Earth.

This perspective has allowed me to see people in a different way. For example, I work with individuals in the medical profession who dedicate their lives to others. Many physicians work very long hours, staying up at night treating people in emergency departments of hospitals, often sacrificing their personal lives for others. I have now started to see how many of these people may be bodhisattvas who incarnated to serve people through medicine.

I asked Ahtun Re about a number of people I knew to find out if they are bodhisattvas, people who may have incarnated voluntarily to help others. One person I asked about is Katarina, a woman in

Serbia who found my website through the Internet and resonated to the message that evidence of reincarnation can help the world become a more peaceful place.

Katarina was attracted in particular to the case of Anne Frank | Barbro Karlen, which demonstrates that people can change religious and ethic affiliation from lifetime to lifetime. Serbia recently fought a war with its neighbor, Croatia, so the lessons of the Frank | Karlen case would have been helpful for that region of the world. If people knew that they could incarnate as a Serb in one lifetime, a Croat in another, a Muslim in one incarnation and Christian in another, then people would not be divided by ethnic or religious affiliation to the same degree. They would have less incentive to fight.

Katarina worked to help get my book *Born Again,* which features the Anne Frank | Barbro Karlen case, published in Serbian. She also facilitated the Serbian publication of Barbro's book, *And the Wolves Howled.* It was clear that her motivation was the desire to help make the world a better place by disseminating information on evidence of reincarnation.

As I learned more about Katarina, it was evident that she is a very evolved soul. She was born in 1954 in Belgrade to poor, lower-class parents. At three years of age, Katarina demonstrated exceptional mathematical skills, which was particularly unusual as she was raised in a rather primitive social setting. When she was in grade school, a special commission was organized at the request of her teacher to examine her special abilities. Though her father was a communist or socialist and speaking about God was forbidden, Katarina knew that God existed even when she was little, though in a form different from what the church portrayed.

At the age of six or seven, Katarina had a premonition in a dream about a disease that she would have at the age of 36, which did in fact occur. This ability to foretell future events became stronger over time, and she has had spontaneous memories of past-life scenes as well. She worked while attending college and started her own business at age 31 that developed into a software company. She was one of the first people to start a business in Serbia after communism fell and she currently employs over 100 people.

When I asked Katarina if it was alright with her if I asked Ahtun Re whether she is a bodhisattva, she agreed, indicating that it does make sense, as she is always doing things for others. Ahtun Re confirmed that Katarina did not have to reincarnate but did so out of choice to help others. Though she is not famous or recognized as a saint by a religious organization, she clearly incarnated with mathematical and organizational skills which exceeded expectations. Given the circumstances of her upbringing, we would surmise that these gifts were acquired in prior incarnations.

Katarina has used her gifts in service, to employ and help others. She has also expressed interest in helping raise funds for www. ReincarnationResearch.com, the organization we have formed to study reincarnation scientifically. She wants to help make the world a better place through the dissemination of objective evidence of reincarnation. So in the example of Katarina, we have an example of a bodhisattva.

Another person who contacted me via the Internet from the other side of the world is Wilja Witcombe, a German national who was working as a business development specialist in Sri Lanka. Wilja too expressed great motivation to help me with reincarnation research in an effort to make the world a better place. Sri Lanka was undergoing a civil war at that time, so again, as in the case of Katarina, there is the hope that evidence of reincarnation will help prevent conflict between groups of differing ethnic and religious affiliation.

Wilja wrote to me as she too has had experiences which seem to stem from a past incarnation, one which occurred in ancient Ceylon, the country which is called Sri Lanka in modern times. Through sessions with Kevin Ryerson and with Ahtun Re's help, the mystery involving Wilja's past lifetime was solved. Though past life images aren't available to compare facial features from one incarnation to another, which would normally be used to corroborate the match, Wilja's story is a good example of how past-life information can unexpectedly come into a person's life and how we are reunited with people we have known and loved in ages past. Let us now turn to Wilja's narrative.

The King and I

Have you ever been told as a child that you are disobedient? That you should behave, "follow protocol," drop a curtsey to guests visiting your parents as well-behaved little girls do (at least at the time I was a kid)? I couldn't see the point that I had to do something like this . . . remembering that "originally" others had to curtsey to me and not vice versa.

To make me comply with what was expected of a well-educated girl, my parents sent me to kindergarten, where I had to curtsey on arrival and departure. I did this to have peace of mind. But do not think that I would have done the curtsey at home – no way!

The same stubbornness I showed with titles. The fact that I refused to use academic, political or aristocratic titles when addressing people annoyed my parents. I especially remembered when we had to meet our family doctor who, following good old German tradition, had to be addressed as "Herr Doktor" and not as "Herr Peterson," as I used to address him.

Whenever my mother took me to the hairdresser as a little girl, she dropped me at the men's section to have my hair cut, not at the ladies.' Whenever "the job" was done and I looked into the mirror to acknowledge my new haircut, the only thought I always had was, "I look like a little fat king again!"

My first piece of jewelry was given to me by my maternal grandma when I was three years old. It was a gold ring over 120 years old with a pinkish stone, handed down from generation to generation. Grandma told me to always remember the name of the stone and where it came from: the stone, so she said, is a padparadscha (belongs to the family of sapphires) and comes from a far-away country called Ceylon. Therefore, Ceylon was the first foreign country I heard about as a child, growing up in post-war Germany.

When I was about 3 years old, my father introduced a young colleague to our family who was the first foreign worker in our small, rural community. The gentleman came from Calcutta in India. He had studied engineering in the UK and had found a job at the company my father was working for as head of the chemical lab. As the young Indian engineer did not speak German at the time and as most of his new colleagues didn't speak any English, my father gave a helping hand, looked after him at work and asked him every weekend to come and join us at home.

Prem had a problem with German food and therefore enjoyed being at our place on Sundays where he would cook "Indian style." He had a small suitcase filled with all kinds of chutneys and spices as well as original tea from the plantation of his brother in Assam. I grew up with the oriental taste of the exotic cuisine from India at an early age – a taste which appealed more to me than the good old German "Hausmannskost."

I was always very fascinated by the gifts our Indian friend would bring back to Germany when he returned from trips to Calcutta. Jewelry and saris for his German wife were just out of this world . . . the colors, the designs, the touch and feel of the materials, the furniture that followed, the rugs, the ornaments . . . something I had seen before . . . I began to feel somehow homesick, but homesick for what?

My parents had given me three first names. Being a girl, they used the female version of my father's name "Klaus" and called me "Claudia." I never felt comfortable with this name. It just wasn't me. The last of the three names was "Wilja," which I always liked best – it felt "me." But of course, as a child, I did not dare to complain about my name and kept quiet.

Years passed. I started school, finished school, started university, finished university, started my business career and started to travel more and more. During the winter season in Europe, I felt the necessity to escape to warmer regions on planet Earth. In 1986 I went for a 6-week holiday to Asia – my first trip to the Far East. I immediately fell in love with Asia, the different countries, people, cultures, religions, customs and traditions. I just couldn't get enough of what this continent had to offer, what it could teach me, and I therefore decided to return to the Far East each year.

At this time, I changed my name to "Wilja"– that made me feel more "me" and "complete," more in sync with my own true self. My environment was amazed but so what? Dare to be different! Live your own life the way you feel it; right!

In May 1997, I visited the Maldives. The hotel director of the holiday resort I stayed at was a very open-hearted man named Rohan, who looked after his guests very well and with a lot of commitment, enthusiasm, passion and joy. I immediately had a warm, comfortable and trustful feeling towards him – a feeling as if I had not seen him for a long, long time, but of course, we had never met before.

When Rohan asked me what I was doing business-wise and I explained the project I was working on at that time, he immediately offered me his help and assistance to explore business opportunities in Sri Lanka, the country he originated from. Although he was working on this tiny atoll in the Indian Ocean, his wife, brother and father would be at my side in Sri Lanka to make introductions and arrange business meetings for me. Everything felt so "normal" and for the first time in my life, I did what I had never done before: I plunged into the "unknown," told him that I would take his offer and go to Sri Lanka in July: he should inform his family and start arranging business meetings.

July came and I left for a 3-week business trip to Colombo, Sri Lanka. I met Rohan's family at the Hotel Intercontinental and immediately fell in love with them all, fell in love with Sri Lanka! For the first time in my life, I felt "at home"– a strange, weird, unknown feeling that I could not understand myself as I had visited over 60 countries, liked most of them, but never had any emotional sensation of this kind.

So it was: I embraced everybody and everything that I encountered. I absorbed the culture, the customs and traditions.

I absorbed Buddhism, was taken to different temples for poojas (religious ceremonies) and was taken to various astrologers and "holy men" to get my future predicted and talismans made to protect me.

I learned about religious ceremonies. Strangely enough, I felt very close to Buddhism on one side, but on the other side (over the following years), I became more critical and sometimes angry with the way Buddhism was practiced. I couldn't understand why I felt so compassionate about this philosophy, but here it was again: this stubbornness from my childhood stopping me to bow or kneel down in front of Buddhist monks (it is called "worshiping") to show respect, to always sit lower than they do, to serve food to them, offer gifts, etc. Something deep inside me was unhappy, or should I say, tried to signal something. I did not understand myself why I balked at this.

Rohan's family was a treasure: they all looked after me like a very close relative that had not been in the country for a long time. They made a lot of introductions, they arranged business meetings, they were always around me to make my stay in Sri Lanka as comfortable, successful and pleasant as possible. When my three weeks were over, I returned to Europe, but I had already scheduled my next visit for September/October of the same year. That was only the start of a series of trips that were to follow over the next five years.

In October 1997, Rohan, who came for a short holiday from the Maldives to see his family, took me for a meeting with the Prime Minister of Sri Lanka, Mrs. Sirimavo Bandaranaike, who was the world's first female Prime Minister in 1960. It was a private meeting at Mrs. Bandaranaike's residence in Colombo and we had a lengthy chat about my experiences of and feelings for Sri Lanka.

Exactly a year later, in October 1998, I met Mrs. Bandaranaike again. This time, it was an official meeting at the Prime Minister's office to discuss charity matters.

When the meeting was over, I was taken to one of the back rooms to wait for my car and driver. In this room one of Mrs. Bandaranaike's private secretaries was seated, an elderly man, sitting at his desk and staring at me in dismay. He could not say a word, he was speechless – he just stared at me with his mouth open, obviously not believing whom or what he was seeing. First, I took it jokingly by asking him if my lipstick or mascara was smudged or upside down, but he still seemed to be flabbergasted and in shock, as if he had seen a ghost. It took me at least 10 minutes to encourage him to talk to me and for him to regain his composure.

When he was finally able and willing to talk, he asked me if I would know who I am. This time, it was I who stared at him. "I think so," I heard me saying. He then asked me, "Have you been to Anuradhapura?" (Anuradhapura is the ancient city of former kings of Sri Lanka. Today only ruins are left of the royal palaces.) "No," I replied, "it is still on my 'to do' list. But why do you ask me that?" And again, the man went silent, just staring at me. It again took me some minutes to persuade him to come up with the next piece of information.

He finally said to me, "I have my Third Eye open and can see the past of a person. I therefore would like you to go to Anuradhapura, alone, and walk around the ruins. You will then feel and know that you once have been one of our ancient kings, and you will be able to identify what part of the palace and buildings had been built during your reign." Now I was stunned and speechless. The secretary did not want to disclose any further information, but insisted that I should go to the ancient city of kings to discover my past.

After this extraordinary encounter, I started to wonder if this man was fantasizing or if there could really be this odd chance of me having been an ancient king of Sri Lanka that was reborn this time as a white female from Europe! At least it would explain my immediate passion for the country, the people, the culture, etc.

*About 6 weeks after this strange meeting at the Prime Min-
ister's office, I was invited to a private event in Colombo, and
destiny repeated itself: this time, an elderly woman looked at
me in disbelief from a distance, and then approached me to tell
me what I had heard before: that I had been one of Ceylon's
ancient kings and have obviously returned to finish "my job"
from the past.*

*So here I was – puzzled, amused, concerned, curious, sur-
prised, wondering, amazed, worried . . . Who was I? What did
these two people see in me? How could they see my past? What
secrets did life keep for me to uncover?*

*Another strange thing happened: since my first visit to Sri
Lanka, I became interested in Ayurveda, the ancient science of
life, i.e. healing. I had various meetings with Ayurvedic doctors and noticed that whenever I introduced myself by saying
"Hi, my name is Wilja," they looked at me a little bit surprised,
though I didn't know why. One day, one Ayurvedic doctor told
me that the way I pronounce my name is Sanskrit, the ancient
language of Asia, and it means "high efficiency"! So here I was
again . . . I do not think that my German parents had any idea
of Sanskrit when they chose this name as one of my first names,
but I am thankful they did!*

*Years passed. I commuted a lot between the UK where I
lived and Sri Lanka, and then decided in 2002 to finally move
to Colombo. Rohan had returned from his assignment in the
Maldives and was now in charge of managing six hotels for
a big Sri Lankan conglomerate. He and his wife had encouraged me to move over and be part of their family. I had a
contract in Sri Lanka for a project to develop, strengthen and
promote two industries of the country. This was something
new to me as I had always been in private industry doing
sales and marketing, but development work was something
that I always wanted to do as a teenager. I started my new
assignment with a lot of joy and passion, always supported
by "my little family."*

Then, life's road took another turn: my dear friend Rohan, while on a business trip to the UK to promote Sri Lanka as a tourist destination, suffered a massive heart attack on the last day of his trip. When the phone call came to inform us about him struggling for his life in a hospital in Birmingham, his wife and two young daughters were living in my house as their new house had not been completed on time and they needed a temporary home. Lekha, his wife, left for the UK. I stayed in Colombo, looking after the children. Rohan's time was up: he died two weeks later, having just turned 43 while being in a coma.

We were all shocked. Was this a bad dream? How could this happen? Why did it happen? Our future was gone! No Rohan, no future!

Now it was my turn to look after the family, after Lekha and the two girls, to help them come to terms with reality, their new lives, paint a picture of a new future. Days turned into weeks, weeks into months, months into years.

I was always wondering what karmic relationship I had with Rohan. It was clear to me that I had known him not only for the seven years we have had together in this lifetime. I was wondering why he had persuaded me to come and visit and then move to Sri Lanka. What was our history, our joint past?

In November 2006, I saw Walter Semkiw's book, Born Again, *in a shop in Colombo. I bought it, read it and sent an email to Walter giving him my feedback, inputs and personal experiences. Walter replied within three days and since then, we have started to communicate and cooperate on the topic of reincarnation. When I mentioned to him my passion for Sri Lanka, I suddenly remembered the two "identifications" of 1998 as an ancient king. Walter volunteered to ask Ahtun Re, the Egyptian spirit guide whom Kevin Ryerson channels, for clarification.*

Some days later, Walter confirmed what the two people had told me in 1998. According to Ahtun Re, I had been an ancient king of Ceylon, one who brought great "spiritual reform" to Ceylon. Ahtun Re had also given some letters of a name but if you have never heard a Sinhalese word, it is difficult to absorb the correct spelling. Ahtun Re said that the name was along the lines of "Devalnu," though the name was an unusual one and the true name could be a variant of Devalnu. Walter explained that even for Ahtun Re, names can be difficult to ascertain precisely, as Ahtun Re perceives them phonetically. In his experience, though, Walter said that Ahtun Re is very accurate in finding a soul in time and place. Walter asked me to do some research and report back to him as he had another session with Kevin/Ahtun Re lined up for the following weekend.

I started my research surfing the Internet that night and downloading a list of all kings of Ceylon of the Anuradhapura period. The next morning, I called up a colleague who had studied Sri Lankan history. When I asked him about a king from Anuradhapura who had brought spiritual reform, he immediately said: "That is King Devanampiya Tissa (reign 247–207 BCE). He introduced Buddhism to this country 2,200 years ago!"

Wow!!! So here I was . . . Now it made sense to me why I fell in love with Sri Lanka and her people immediately and why I was so skeptical about the practical side of Buddhism in Sri Lanka.

I sent an email to Walter with all the necessary details and within a week, I had his, i.e. Ahtun Re's positive feedback: yes, King Devanampiya Tissa was the ancient king I had been once before. Walter noted that Ahtun Re did get the first part of the name right with the letters "Deva-n." No other king of Ceylon has a name that starts with this combination of letters.

Now came the next piece of the puzzle: who was Rohan before? He must have been part of my "royal life." That was absolutely certain to me. I started to read as much as I could on King Devanampiya Tissa and also booked a telephone session with Kevin Ryerson/Ahtun Re.

A couple of days before the session, I found the piece of information I was looking for: King Devanampiya Tissa was married and had a little son. His wife, whose name is not known, was jealous that in case of his early death, one of his brothers would take over the throne instead of their son. To assure her son's right to the throne, the wife decided to kill Tissa's brother by sending him a basket of ripe mangoes. She poisoned the biggest, nicest and shiniest mango and put it on top of the basket. When the brother received the basket, Tissa's young son was with him. The son took the top mango, ate it and died.

This was my realization. I intuitively knew who Rohan had been: I had known him for only 7 years in this lifetime, the lifespan of a child . . . Rohan had been King Devanampiya Tissa's son – my son!

When I had the telephone session with Kevin, I asked Ahtun Re what karmic relationship I had with Rohan. Ahtun Re immediately confirmed what I had found out some days earlier: that Rohan was King Devanampiya Tissa's young, innocent son who was poisoned by his own mother and died!

Now I understand the saying: death ends a life, not a relationship!

So, here I am: living in Sri Lanka, looking after Rohan's widow and my karmic great great, great, great grandchildren! Is the karmic lifecycle now complete? I don't know.

I do now see and understand the hints and signs destiny had provided throughout my life: my first piece of jewelry with the padparadscha stone from Ceylon, my identification with a Sanskrit name, my early introduction to spicy, Indian food and Asian culture, were all part of my preparation for what was to come later in life; my rejection of "obedience" as a child when it came to "behaving properly," my love for Asia. . . .

Each day is full of surprises, something new, more challenges, and the unexpected! I feel that there is more to come. . . . The future has just started, and I am embracing everything that surfaces as I am more and more spiritually open and prepared for it!

In Wilja's narrative, we see how she received unconscious clues about her past incarnation, such as when, after she had a haircut as a child, she saw herself once again as a fat little king. Wilja has also expressed an enthusiastic desire to help www.Reincarnation Research.com to develop. Just as King Devanampiya Tissa brought spiritual reform to ancient Ceylon, Wilja, by supporting reincarnation research, demonstrates the same urge to enact spiritual reform today. Lastly, I would like to point out that in my experience of Wilja, the Sanskrit name she chose for herself, which means "high efficiency," is very apt, for Wilja is an organized dynamo.

Belief versus Knowledge: Reincarnation and the Civil War in Sri Lanka

There is a poignant aspect to Wilja's story. In the civil war that was fought in Sri Lanka, the island that was once known as Ceylon, both sides in the conflict, the Sinhalese Buddhist majority and the Hindu minority, the Tamils, believe in reincarnation. This raises the important point that just believing in reincarnation is not sufficient to bring peace.

Believing in something is different from knowing that something is true. With beliefs, we do not always follow the precepts of the belief system, as there is still a level of uncertainty. As an example, if you are driving down the highway and you don't see a policeman, you may be tempted to exceed the speed limit. Who doesn't? On the other hand, if you are driving and you see a policeman right behind you in your rear view mirror, you become very obedient regarding traffic laws. In the same way, there is a difference in believing in reincarnation and knowing that it is true. Knowing that you are accountable for your actions creates a different mindset.

When people know that reincarnation is true and understand, as demonstrated in the Anne Frank | Barbro Karlen case, that religion, ethic affiliation and nationality can change from lifetime to lifetime, then behavior will change. When the Sinhalese Buddhist knows, without a doubt, that he or she can reincarnate as a Tamil Hindu and vice versa, then the motivation to fight will be lessened.

In a session with Kevin Ryerson, I asked Ahtun Re whether Wilja is also a bodhisattva, one who reincarnated voluntarily to serve. Ahtun Re related that this is true. Perhaps Wilja returned, in part, to help take care of Rohan's family. Another form of service Wilja is very invested in is that she wants to help small and medium-sized enterprises in Sri Lanka become more professional and efficient, thereby making them more competitive in the world market. She has also created an organization to help people develop work skills; she has created livelihood projects at the grass-roots level. She wants to be a bridge-builder between East and West, between ancient wisdom and contemporary thought. In this light, perhaps Wilja, like Katarina, has returned to help bring objective evidence of reincarnation into the world.

We see, through the examples of Katarina and Wilja, that bodhisattvas are all around us. When I reflect on the anxieties that plague our modern world, it is a great comfort to me to know that so many bodhisattvas have returned.

14

Past Lives of Jesus, the Holocaust, Initiation, Ascension and Forgiveness

We have reviewed levels of development of the human soul, as well as strata of the spiritual world. In an effort to better understand these concepts in the context of a person considered by Christians to the most highly evolved being who has ever lived, I asked Ahtun Re, the spirit guide channeled by Kevin Ryerson, about past lives of Jesus. I also asked Ahtun Re to comment on levels of initiation, as described in Theosophical literature. Recall that Ahtun Re has demonstrated the ability to make accurate past-life matches, which to me, gives him a level of credibility. Also recall that Ahtun Re has stated that he served as a spirit guide to Jesus during his ministry on Earth which led to the crucifixion and resurrection. Ahtun Re himself last incarnated in Egypt over 3,000 years ago.

In addition, I have asked Wayne Peterson to contribute an essay on reincarnation and initiation, for he is a scholar in these areas. Wayne is featured in *Born Again,* in which three of his past lives are described. A retired US Diplomat and former Director of the Fulbright Scholarship Program in Washington, DC, Wayne brings direct experience into the discussion, for he has personally interacted with spiritual masters like Jesus, Maitreya and Saint Germain, who have materialized before him in experiences spanning over 30 years. As Wayne relates in his book, *Extraordinary Times, Extraordinary Beings,* those who we call Initiates, Ascended Masters or Masters of Wisdom are very real to him, and Wayne even calls some of them his friends.

Edgar Cayce and Past Lives of Jesus

Let us now turn to past lifetimes of Jesus. Ahtun Re has told me that Jesus had a total of 33 incarnations, culminating in the lifetime in which he was known as Jesus of Nazareth. Previously, Ahtun Re estimated that for most of us, 80 to 120 incarnations are needed before the cycle of Earthly reincarnation ends, so I asked Ahtun Re how Jesus attained mastery in only 33 lifetimes.

As explained in a prior chapter, universes existed prior to our universe, which was created in the Big Bang about 14 billion years ago. Souls evolved on these previous universes and a certain group volunteered to be part of our universe. So 14 billion years ago, a group of experienced souls emerged into our universe, a soul group of about 144,000, to join the souls who were newly-created a nano-second or so after our Big Bang.

This group of experienced souls volunteered to serve, as well as lead humanity, and according to Ahtun Re many of our great spiritual figures like the Buddha, Moses, Mohammed, Jesus, the great Swamis of Hinduism, as well as individuals of genius, were part of this group. Given their prior experience in a universe that existed before ours, they were able to accomplish more in a fewer number of lives.

Edgar Cayce, who lived from 1877 to 1945, became one of the most famous mediums in history. Like Kevin Ryerson, Cayce would go into a meditative trance during which he would channel information that was outside of Cayce's own fund of knowledge. Most of his readings focused on providing remedies for individuals with health problems. Cayce founded the Association for Research and Enlightenment (ARE), which is still active, with centers found in more than 35 countries.

Many of Cayce's channelings involve reincarnation, a topic that he himself was initially resistant to, as Edgar Cayce was a devout Christian. Further, his channelings described multiple past incarnations of Jesus. Ahtun Re has indicated that the majority of the information that Cayce provided on past lives of Jesus is accurate.

A book that reviews these past lives in detail was written by Glenn Sandefur and entitled, *Lives of the Master*. I would like to review two of these past lives of Jesus as proposed in the Cayce material, one that is easy to accept and another that is more troubling and perplexing.

Jesus as the Reincarnation of Joseph with the Coat of Many Colors

One past lifetime of Jesus that I would like to share involves the biblical figure Joseph, who was given a coat of many colors by his father, Jacob. Though there is no way of precisely determining when Joseph lived, it is thought that this incarnation occurred about 1,700 years BC.

Joseph was known to have a gift for dream interpretation. In the Old Testament, it is written that he had two brothers who were jealous of him, as it seemed that Jacob loved Joseph more than them. Joseph told his brother of two dreams in which he was elevated over them, which irked the brothers even more. As a result, they conspired to sell Joseph into slavery in Egypt.

Joseph's master in Egypt, whose name was Putiphar, recognized talent in Joseph, who eventually was given charge of the household. Putiphar's wife was attracted to Joseph and tried to seduce him. When he rejected her advances, the wife, in anger, told Putiphar that Joseph had seduced her, who believed his wife's lie and placed Joseph in prison.

In prison, Joseph met the Pharaoh's chief butler and chief baker, who were incarcerated for unknown reasons. Joseph correctly interpreted dreams the butler and baker had, and when they were released, they brought Joseph's dream interpretation gifts to the attention of the Pharaoh, who was perplexed by a dream that he had had of a fat cow and a lean cow.

Joseph interpreted the Pharaoh's dream to mean Egypt would go through seven years of prosperity followed by seven years of famine. Joseph advised that grain should be stored during the seven years of prosperity, which would be used to feed the population during the time of famine.

The Pharaoh followed the advice of Joseph and these things did come to pass, making Joseph a hero to the Egyptians. Eventually, Joseph's brothers came to Egypt at behest of their father to obtain food for their family during the famine. With his brothers being brought before him, Joseph's dream of being elevated above his brothers was fulfilled. Joseph eventually forgave his brothers and the family was reunited.

In having to go through the ordeal of being sold into slavery and then being imprisoned, followed by the redemption of Joseph and his practice of forgiveness, Joseph has been considered by scholars to be a Jesus-like figure.

Jesus as the Reincarnation of Joshua

Another past incarnation of Jesus, according to the Cayce material, was that of Joshua, who was an assistant to Moses during the Exodus and then became the leader of the Israelites or Hebrews after Moses died. Joshua led the Hebrews in the conquest of the lands of Canaan, which in modern times is known as Israel. It is believed that Joshua lived sometime around 1400 BC.

The troubling aspect about this proposed past lifetime is that Joshua has been depicted, in the Bible, as a ruthless warrior. Joshua led the Israelites in the battle of Jericho, where the walls of the city purportedly fell after the Israelite army marched around the city blowing their trumpets. Some modern scholars believe that the walls did not literally fall, but that the blowing of the trumpets provided a distraction which allowed Israelite commandos to secretly penetrate Jericho's defenses. According to the Bible, Jericho was completely destroyed and every man, woman and child was killed.

Joshua and the Israelites later fought the Amorites, a Semitic ethnic group that inhabited the highlands of Canaan. The Amorites were described by historians as "white skinned, blue eyed, fair haired." Another description follows: "The Amorites . . . were a tall, handsome people, with white skins, blue eyes and reddish hair, all the characteristics, in fact, of the white race."[1]

The Amorites had five kings corresponding to their five territories, those of Jerusalem, Hebron, Jarmuth, Lachish and Eglon. When Joshua and his forces defeated the Amorites, the five kings hid in a cave in the city of Mekkedah. When the five kings were found, the Bible indicates that Joshua had them brought before him and he then summoned his army in order to humiliate the kings. He then had his commanders put their feet on the necks of the kings. Joshua then killed the kings and had them hung on five trees.

The difficulty in accepting Joshua as a previous incarnation of Jesus is that Jesus is perceived as sacrificing himself for others: for preaching forgiveness and nonviolence. How could Jesus have been so ruthless in a lifetime as Joshua, which occurred only 1400 years before that of Jesus?

Glenn Sandefur, the author of *Lives of the Master*, was also perplexed by this proposed past lifetime of Jesus, which was contained in the Cayce material. He tried to reconcile the paradox by hypothesizing that the death of Jesus by crucifixion was a karmic consequence of the slaughter performed by Joshua and the manner in which Joshua disposed of the five kings by humiliating them, killing them and then hanging them from five trees. Sandefur noted that being crucified on a wooden cross could be seen as a reflection of Joshua hanging the kings from trees.

This karmic explanation initially also appealed to me, as I never understood why Jesus had to go through the crucifixion. After all, what made his legacy was his resurrection, not his death. If Jesus had lived a long and happy life, died by natural means and then resurrected, his legacy would have been just as great. Further, other founders of religions, such as Buddha and Mohammed, did not undergo torturous deaths, so why did Jesus?

Due to my problems with the proposed past lifetime of Jesus as Joshua and my questions regarding the crucifixion, I asked Ahtun Re for his insights on these matters. First of all, Ahtun Re stated that the biblical account of Joshua and his actions is not fully accurate.

Joshua did not slaughter the populations of his enemies as depicted in the Bible. Rather, those who wrote these accounts exaggerated the violence involved as a warning to other tribes who may challenge the Israelites in the future. In reality, Ahtun Re said that Joshua allowed enemy survivors of battles to leave, rather than be killed, which was a very enlightened manner of conducting warfare for that time.

Ahtun Re pointed out that the Amorite kings were inhumane leaders who even practiced human sacrifice. The Israelites considered Canaan as their ancestral home which they were displaced from and in taking Canaan, they were reclaiming land that was originally theirs. Ahtun Re stated that Joshua taking Canaan as comparable to Dwight Eisenhower liberating France.

Ahtun Re also stated that the five kings were not promptly executed in the manner described in the Bible. Rather, there were trials of the five kings which Ahtun Re stated were akin to the Nuremberg trials. Ahtun Re said that the five kings were "guilty as sin." Joshua did preside over the trials and executions of the kings.

Ahtun Re shared that being a military leader was an atypical role for the soul of Jesus. If we use the model of the Seven Rays, Jesus has been identified as a Sixth Ray soul. As such, in most of his lifetimes, Jesus was involved in various forms of religious devotion. He was typically a temple priest, a rabbi or other religious leader. Ahtun Re noted that the Joshua lifetime was a difficult one for the soul of Jesus, but he pursued it as he was devoted to Moses and his Hebrew tribe.

The Five Kings, the Crucifixion and the Jewish Holocaust

I asked Ahtun Re about the identities of the five kings and what karmic connections they may have had with Jesus. It turned out that these kings not only had karmic connections with Jesus, but some were involved in the Holocaust of World War II. Recall that the Amorites were described as a tall, fair skinned and blue-eyed people who embodied the appearance of the Caucasian race. In other words, the Amorites had the same physical appearance as the Nazis' ideal Aryan race.

The identities of the five Amorite kings of Canaan, in relation to subsequent incarnations, are as follows, according to Ahtun Re.

- The King of Jerusalem in the era of Joshua was the soul of Adolph Hitler, who reincarnated in the time of Jesus as King Herod. Ahtun Re said that the soul of Hitler incarnated as Herod to better understand Jewish culture.

- The King of Hebron was the soul of the Nazi leader Joseph Goebbels, who as the King of Hebron implemented a spy and propaganda system in which neighbors would turn in neighbors for monetary reward. This soul of Goebbels reincarnated in the era of Jesus as a Roman senator who sponsored Herod's rule.

- The King of Eglon was the soul of Benito Mussolini, who reincarnated in the era of Jesus as the son of Herod | Hitler.

- The King of Lachish was the soul of Judas, who as the King of Canaan imposed a ruthless tax collection system. He too incarnated as a Jew to learn of the culture, but also to help equalize karma between he and Joshua | Jesus. By mentoring Judas, Jesus was creating positive karma with Judas. Judas betrayed Jesus as he wanted Jesus to use his spiritual powers to become a King of the Jews in a physical sense, to overthrow the Romans and to create a Jewish state. In hanging himself from a tree after the crucifixion, Judas reenacted being hung from a tree as the King of Lachish.

- The King of Jarmuth was the soul of Joseph Stalin, who reincarnated as a Roman general during the time of Jesus, who eventually came to know the Apostle Paul. Though the soul of Stalin in the era of Jesus participated in the destruction of Jerusalem, he later became a convert.

Was the Crucifixion Karmic in Origin?

I asked Ahtun Re about the question raised by Glenn Sandefur as to whether the crucifixion of Jesus was related to how Joshua had the five kings hung from trees. Ahtun Re stated that by the time Jesus was born, he had neutralized all karma from his previous lives.

Ahtun Re stated that the karma of Jesus at the time of this birth was "squeaky clean." One way that he did this is that the soul of Jesus had two lifetimes following that of Joshua in which he incarnated into tribes that were enemies of the Israelites. In these two lifetimes, Joshua | Jesus was killed by Hebrew soldiers. The soul of Jesus also neutralized karma through good works performed in lifetimes subsequent to Joshua.

Ahtun Re indicated that there was a connection between the killing of the five kings and the crucifixion of Jesus, but it was not due to the karma of Jesus. Rather, the connection was due to unconscious resentments that the reincarnated Amorite kings had against Jesus. The King of Jerusalem | King Herod | Adolph Hitler, the King of Eglon | son of Herod | Mussolini and the King of Lachish | Judas all subconsciously wanted Jesus to undergo the same fate that they felt he had imposed on them when they were Amorite kings. Ironically, Ahtun Re noted that after the crucifixion, when Judas hung himself from a tree in grief, he replicating his death as the King of Lachish.

The Amorite Kings and the Holocaust

Just as past-life resentments were associated to the crucifixion of Jesus, these same past-life resentments contributed to the Holocaust of World War II. Two leaders of the Nazi party in Germany were two of the Amorite kings. Adolf Hitler was identified as the King of Jerusalem during the time of Joshua, as well as King Herod in the time of Jesus. Joseph Goebbels was identified as the King of Hebron, who later reincarnated as a Roman senator who sponsored King Herod | Adolph Hitler.

Hitler and Goebbels still held on to these unconscious resentments from their lives as Amorite kings, in which the Israelites or Hebrews conquered them and executed them. This led to their hatred of Jews in their lives during World War II. Their glorification of the Aryan race reflects their attachment to their lives as Amorites, who were described as tall, blue-eyed and fair skinned.

These unconscious resentments do not justify their hatred for Jews or the Holocaust, for recall that Ahtun Re stated that the Amorite kings were ruthless leaders who were "guilty as sin." This narrative, if accepted, does demonstrate how violence leads to resentments which lead to further cycles of violence. Through forgiveness and understanding ourselves through reincarnation, by seeing ourselves as universal humans who do not overly identified with any particular nation, religion, ethnic affiliation or tribe, we can prevent cycles of violence from recurring.

Can the Karma of Genocide Be Neutralized?

I asked Ahtun Re what will happen to souls such as Hitler, who are responsible for genocide. First of all, Hitler will need to go through a series of lifetimes where he is the victim and he will have to endure what he did to others. Another way that Hitler can redeem himself is by creating a positive impact on mass consciousness in the same degree that he created a negative impact during World War II. After Hitler endures victim lifetimes, he can reincarnate and use his leadership abilities to create positive actions, which affect millions of people in a beneficial way.

Ahtun Re predicts that the five kings will indeed redeem themselves in future incarnations, in part because they will reincarnate in a more evolved society and world. Objective evidence of reincarnation will be one of the catalysts for creating this more evolved world.

The important point to remember is that even Jesus went through a process of development, through reincarnation, as we all do. In his 33rd incarnation, in becoming Jesus Christ, Jesus attained a certain level of initiation, for the term Christ can be understood to be a title, indicating a level of spiritual accomplishment. We are all destined to follow his path. This brings us to our next topic, that of initiation.

Initiation

To better understand the concept of initiation, I would like to return to an idea raised before, in which we envision that a soul has the capability to project holograms of itself. It was noted that we can understand how facial features remain consistent from one incarnation to another by envisioning the soul projecting a three-dimensional hologram of itself into the developing physical body. Our facial architecture is a mathematical property of the soul. The hologram serves as an invisible energy template that bone and tissue develop around, and which results in our unique facial architecture manifesting from lifetime to lifetime.

The idea of the hologram was also used to understand how split incarnation can occur, in that a soul, as it becomes more proficient through repeated incarnations, can project several holograms of itself into several physical bodies at one time. We also used the hologram to understand the phenomenon of child prodigies like Alexandra Nechita, who demonstrated the talent of Picasso at a very young age. We can imagine the soul of Picasso projecting a hologram into Alexandra's body, not only shaping bone structure and facial features, but also downloading the talent of Picasso into her young mind.

In this section, we will consider that with higher levels of initiation, the soul is able to project more complex and refined holograms into the physical plane, holograms that are as real as physical bodies, though they are made of pure energy. We will call these holograms "bodies of light," or alternately, "light bodies."

As mentioned, Wayne Peterson has witnessed spiritual masters manifesting in light bodies over a period of 30 years. In fact, the spiritual masters Maitreya and Jesus once appeared to him together on Rodeo Drive, in Beverly Hills, California. Wayne was in Beverly Hills, coincidentally, to attend an art exhibition of Alexandra Nechita. In his book, Wayne describes several incidents involving ascended beings who materialize. All of these encounters are amazing and some are quite amusing.

One of my favorite stories, which is featured in *Extraordinary Times, Extraordinary Beings,* is the one that occurred when Wayne was staying in Honolulu after inspecting US embassies in Asia for the Fulbright Program. Wayne relates that late at night, he spotted a spirit being with golden hair appear in the fronds of a palm tree, who then floated over to his balcony and into his hotel room. A few seconds later, the spiritual master Saint Germain appeared, wearing a violet sash. Saint Germain instructed Wayne to listen to the younger master with the golden hair. Saint Germain then smiled, winked and disappeared. Wayne, quite shocked, started pinching himself to make sure he wasn't sleeping and dreaming. Finding that he was awake, he then listened to the being with golden hair give a discourse on self-realization.

Afterwards, Wayne himself found the experience hard to believe and he wished he had been given some tangible token, some physical object, which would validate that the experience in Hawaii with these masters was real. When Wayne was back in Washington, the spiritual masters complied and gave him a token as big as a tree. Refer to Wayne's book to learn more.

Let me share another story from Wayne involving spiritual masters and light bodies. The master he is most in touch with is called Maitreya, who typically appears as a very tall, thin man with an olive complexion and who likes to wear unusual hats. A peculiar property of his hats is that when different people look at Maitreya at the same time, at presentations and book signings that Wayne has done, they all see a hat, but each person sees a different-shaped hat. Another characteristic of Maitreya, by the way, is that he is playful and demonstrates a sense of humor.

In January 2007, Wayne's neighbor, a nice lady who had recently read his book, had to go to her doctor. It was early in the morning and she was the only one in the waiting room. After registering, she turned around and saw a tall, thin man with an olive complexion, wearing a white hat and standing in the waiting room reading Wayne's book *Extraordinary Times, Extraordinary Beings*. Excited, the lady ran up to him and exclaimed, "My neighbor wrote that book!"

The tall man in the white hat ignored her remark and simply stated, "This is a good book. More people should be reading it." The lady was then called by the receptionist to be taken to the exam room to be evaluated by her doctor, but before she went in, she turned around to ask the tall man how he came across Wayne's book. The man, however, had disappeared. When the neighbor lady told Wayne of this event, he explained that she had surely seen Maitreya, whom Wayne has similarly encountered in many unexpected settings.

One more point of interest is that Wayne Peterson had the opportunity to present his experiences with spiritual masters, who can manifest in light bodies, to a Vatican delegation visiting Washington. DC. Wayne presented for over three hours and the head of the delegation was Joseph Ratzinger, who was a very close advisor to the Pope at that time, John Paul II. Joseph Ratzinger later became Pope Benedict XVI. After Wayne's presentation, Cardinal Ratzinger revealed that John Paul II knew of these phenomena, but that it was for the Holy Father to determine whether they should be discussed publicly.

Let us now review a model of initiation. Theosophy describes nine levels of initiation, though only the first five pertain to human beings. I will use terms that Wayne has used in his narrative, which is provided below, to describe the levels of initiation as symbolically enacted in events in the life of Jesus. I have added comments from Ahtun Re, where appropriate.

> Probationary Path: This is a level that precedes the first initiation, in which the material world is the primary focus of the individual. According to Theosophy, most of humanity is still in the probationary stage.
>
> Initiation 1, Birth: The soul commands the personality to pay more attention to the spiritual life than to the material.
>
> Initiation 2, The Baptism: The personality overcomes illusion, in that the incarnated being understands that its identity is not based in matter or the physical world.
>
> Initiation 3, The Transfiguration on the Mount: The soul is totally in command and the personality lives by soul direction.
>
> Initiation 4, The Crucifixion: In this stage, the personality gives up all attachments to material life and completely

focuses on spiritual matters, sacrificing itself for all humanity. Ahtun Re has indicated that Jesus, in his past lifetime as Joseph with the coat of many colors, was a level 4 initiate.

Initiation 5, The Resurrection: The soul can take on a body of light on the physical plane.

In Christian theology, the Ascension is described as Jesus, in bodily form, rising up to heaven. By using the analogy of the hologram, we can better visualize how the process of Ascension may have taken place. Ascension is simply the soul's ability to create a hologram, a body of light that takes on the quality of physical reality. Whereas Level 5 initiation brings with it the development of such a body of light, Ahtun Re explains that higher levels of initiation involve achieving greater mastery in utilizing a body of light. Ahtun Re suggests that with his resurrection, Jesus actually attained higher levels of initiation.

An interesting feature of light bodies is that there can be varying levels of consolidation or density. Recall that according to the Gospel of John, after the crucifixion, when Jesus first appears to Mary Magdalene outside the tomb, he instructs her, "Do not touch me, for I have not yet ascended to the Father."

Wayne Peterson has had similar experiences with Maitreya, where Wayne, at times, has not been allowed to touch the light body of Maitreya. At these times, Maitreya's body will even retreat in a blink of an eye. At other times, the light body of a master spiritual being will appear as real as the flesh and blood of any human being. Wayne explains that producing a physically dense light body takes a great deal of energy. As such, masters do so only when it is necessary. Let us now turn to Wayne's essay on reincarnation and initiation:

Why Do We Reincarnate?

The short answer to this question is that the soul insists upon reincarnation in order to perfect its connection with the human personality. The biblical text wisely includes an important statement regarding the need for reincarnation. St. Paul phrased it for us, "Whatsoever a man soweth, that shall he also reap." (Gal. VI: 7). It is a truth that needs re-emphasizing. This is also called the Law of Cause and Effect. In the Eastern world it is called simply the Law of Karma.

The emphasis of the teachings of Jesus was about the goal of right human relations. Therefore, his teachings must be tied to the Law of Rebirth. In order for the human personality to reap what it has sowed, it would take far more than one life period. It is a process which we call evolution of the human spirit, a process of perfecting the human soul. Jesus told us, "Be ye, therefore, perfect, even as your Father which is in Heaven is perfect." (Matt. V: 48). As we progress upon our spiritual journey, we learn how to perfect ourselves, just as Jesus was an outstanding example.

Today, average humanity is far more perfected than our forefathers were. We cannot even begin to imagine the cruelty of the human race over tens of thousands of years. We can imagine the inhumanity to man during our last hundred years, which included the great world wars. Huge amounts of negative karma were placed on the heads of much of humanity. Yet, those evil-doing lives or souls have to become perfected. This could only happen if the Law of Rebirth existed. When the disciples asked Christ about the blind man, "Master, did this man sin or his fathers that he was born blind?" (John IX: 2), the church leaders too often simply brush it aside as if the statement did not matter or even relate to reincarnation. On the opposite side, those who accept reincarnation as a fact have presented their case to the public in a deplorable manner. It needs to be more intelligently presented, especially in the West.

In the last analysis, if perfection is to be ultimately achieved, the question is merely one of time and location. Although the purification process is thought by some opponents of reincarnation to take place outside the Earthly life, the teachings have never been very convincing to most. If spiritual evolution is necessary to purify the soul, then it is most logical that it continues here.

Why? Because how else can we reap what we have sown in those cases when we harmed our neighbor? We can only correct a wrong to our neighbor by dealing directly with the person we have harmed. This brings us to the esoteric fact that reincarnation is not about individuals but about groups of souls.

Humanity has slowly accepted the idea that we are immortal beings. Unfortunately, the mainstream religions have given humanity a very distorted look at our choices. The Western religions have us coming from a non-existent past with only a present-time life and a future of a boring heaven or a terrible suffering for eternity, with all of this supposedly occurring under the direction of a loving God. It is no wonder that many have turned away from such simplistic and distorted views. An intelligent understanding of the journey of the human soul and its perfection is needed before reincarnation can be clearly visualized and accepted by humanity. It will be the study of groups of souls coming into incarnation with a rational plan to deal with the Law of Karma that will convince intelligent people that reincarnation is a fact of life.

The fact is that souls reincarnate in groups in order to perfect the relationships between them. It would do no good for the soul to be reincarnated into a family and friends group where that soul had no karmic debt. We can only pay back our debt to others we have harmed in the past if we can encounter them again and again until we have that relationship perfected. Therefore, our current family and friends have known each other for eons of time. That process will continue until the karma has been neutralized. At that time, advanced souls will begin to take on racial karma, national karma, world karma and focus on service to all humanity. These souls are the saints of old and the modern-day world servers.

The advanced soul, one who has neutralized most of his karmic debt within his family and friends, can then begin to deal with world karma and often then chooses to reincarnate into a totally new family of previously unrelated souls. He will, nevertheless,

continue to recognize his old friends who have perfected them-
selves along with him over the past centuries. When he meets them
in the workplace or through social gatherings, he will recognize
them as a dear old friend and will wish to maintain that contact.
The karmic debt of the advanced soul is now gone and the two
individuals can exist in a loving relationship and mutual support.
They will notice that each of them has chosen a path of service to
humanity and they are active in the larger world, not just within
a small circle of family and friends. It is these advanced groups
of souls, now off on a very individual journey of service, that can
be most easily traced back into history. Their group relationships
and group reincarnations will be the light that shines upon this
topic and brings meaning to reincarnation for humanity.

We too often overlook the important fact that service and
sacrifice by advanced souls is a key to understanding reincar-
nation. Jesus taught humanity about service and sacrifice just
as so many great souls before him did also. Lord Buddha, Lord
Krishna or Christna, Mithra of Persia or Osiris of Egypt all
sacrificed for the less evolved souls. They, and many more, were
examples to humanity. They led the way and showed the path.
We are expected to be someday like them, to be heroes to human-
ity before we pass on to greater work beyond this planet.

What is important to understand about reincarnation on
our planet is that when the soul is perfected, we too will follow
in the steps of those great heroes who have gone before us. We
will complete what the secret societies of the past taught about
the five initiations which take place through incarnations on
Earth. These five initiations were taught by Jesus with his life.
They are performed in the last few lives of a human soul on this
planet. Jesus performed the initiations in a physical manner
which ended in his resurrection.

The first initiation is the Birth, the process when the soul
commands the personality to pay more attention to the spiritual
life than to the material. The second is the Baptism, the point
when the soul overcomes illusion. The third is the Transfiguration

on the Mount, the moment when the soul is totally in command and a man lives by soul direction. The fourth, the Crucifixion, is when humans give up all attachments to material life, focus on spiritual matters and sacrifice for all humanity. The last is Resurrection from the dead and taking on a body of light. This usually ends our Earthly journey. It is then that the fifth-degree initiate has a choice of seven paths into a new journey of adventure in the vast universe. Unlike our Earthly journey, the universal journey of our soul will be without pain and suffering of any sort. It will be a journey of great joy. It will, nevertheless, be a journey of continued evolution of the spirit.

I wish to make it known that these ideas are not my own. The teachings come from a human soul who has suffered the human journey and passed through the five initiations to become enlightened. For whatever reason, he remained on our planet to teach humanity about our destiny. He is often called simply the Tibetan Master. He worked with Alice Bailey for a period of over thirty years to place into books all the information advanced humanity would require at this time to find our path to enlightenment as fast as possible. Humanity owes him a great thank you. I consider him my friend.

My final thought is that it is very important that we see reincarnation as a process to bring the human soul to perfection. This evolutionary journey always proceeds forward, never backwards. Teachings that would have us believe that our spiritual journey could ever move backwards are simply religious leaders attempting to hold humanity in their control for selfish purposes. The Law of Rebirth and its purpose to perfect the human soul is fact, and works in harmony with the teachings of Jesus and earlier great world teachers.

The Crucifixion and Forgiveness

One of the most powerful elements of the story of Jesus is that he had the ability to forgive even those who were crucifying him. My understanding of this is that he lived on a higher level of spiritual reality, where events of the physical world, including his own death, were not meaningful for him. Further, he knew that he was part of a great demonstration in which he would show the world that death could be overcome though self sacrifice, through sacrifice of the ego. He became a model for souls such as Gandhi and Martin Luther King. And so Jesus did overcome death and the crucifix has become his universal symbol.

Forgiveness was a central message of Jesus. The reason, I believe, that forgiveness is so important is that by holding on to resentments, we bind ourselves into karmic relationships with those we harbor anger or resentment towards. We get stuck in our soul development. By forgiving, we free ourselves, we let go of an anchor that holds us back.

Forgiveness, though, can be very difficult. Though some, such as those who study the *Course in Miracles*, advocate that forgiveness can occur by conceiving that the offense never occurred, for most of us, working through emotions associated with our wounds is required for forgiveness to be complete. If we do not work through these emotions, resentments can multiply. First of all, the victim has pain from being wounded by a perpetrator. Secondly, the victim, if unable to readily forgive, feels guilty for not being able to forgive. It seems doubly unfair, as the perpetrator doesn't have to struggle with the issue of forgiveness. A downward, obsessive spiral of negativity, pain and resentment can ensue.

As a practical matter, it is most effective to communicate with the perpetrator of a wound, perhaps in a letter, to explain how that person's actions caused you pain. Ask that the perpetrator empathize and apologize, explaining that an apology would constitute a therapeutic act. If the perpetrator can empathize, healing and forgiveness can take place. If the perpetrator cannot empathize and apologize, the act of communicating one's feelings is in itself cathartic. Traditional psychotherapy may also be of great help.

What if the perpetrator is no longer alive? I asked Ahtun Re this, and he encouraged that the same process be done. One should still write down emotions related to wounds and ask that the perpetrator empathize and apologize. Ahtun Re pointed out that even if a person has died, that person's soul will still be available to you through telepathic communication. He pointed out that the individual in question may even appear to you in dreams. Indeed, as an example of this phenomenon, a close friend of mine revealed that when her grandmother died, who exhibited cruelty to my friend, the deceased grandmother appeared to her in a dream which seemed very, very real, asking that my friend forgive her.

Jack Kornfield has written a useful book entitled *The Art of Forgiveness, Lovingkindness and Peace,* in which he too relates that forgiveness can be a long, difficult process. In the end, though, it is we who are freed by it. Jack illustrates this in a dialogue between two former prisoners of war. One states to the other, "Have you forgiven your captors yet?" The other says, "No, never!" The first replies, "Well then, they still have you in prison, don't they."[2] Another important step in achieving forgiveness is recognizing that it doesn't help to obsess over the past. He writes, "Forgiveness means giving up hope for a better past."[3]

Let me add one other perspective. I myself have trouble with the term forgiveness, as it implies the continuation of a relationship. I prefer the word "detachment," as it conveys that one does not carry negative emotions associated with the perpetrator of wrongdoing and in addition, allows the person who was hurt to release the relationship and be free. Detachment conveys that one releases emotional wounds that the perpetrator caused with the knowledge that karma will do its work. With detachment, one can truly let go of the perpetrator and related wounds and allow paths to diverge.

One of the lessons of the crucifixion is that in this world, there will always be those who wound. Lesser evolved souls will have a tendency to wound more advanced souls. Wayne Peterson alluded to this in his essay. Just as Jesus chose forgiveness and initiation, so must we if we want to attain higher levels of spiritual awareness and become master hologram makers.

Michael Tamura is a clairvoyant and spiritual teacher who has helped me with my own struggles with forgiveness. Michael, by the way, recalls a lifetime in which he was a disciple of Jesus and he relates that in clairvoyant states, Jesus visits him often. Other clairvoyants, who have contributed to this book, including Echo Bodine and Judy Goodman, also receive visits from Jesus.

Uniformly, in contrast to traditional portrayals, Michael, Echo and Judy describe Jesus as lighthearted and joyful, someone who likes to make them laugh with little jokes. Another friend who experiences Jesus as a great energy of love relates that Jesus has told him that he wants to be taken off that cross, as he has progressed far beyond that moment in time. Let me now conclude with lines written by Michael Tamura:

> *"God never changes. It is only we who must change our ways if we are to join in that everlasting bliss. With every step of forgiveness, the journey of a thousand deaths heals into eternal, joyous life – and peace."*

To learn more, go to:

www.MichaelTamura.com

15

Conclusion

In the chapters of this book, as well as in *Born Again* and *Return of the Revolutionaries,* we have traversed a great deal of territory. We have reviewed compelling cases in which children report memories of past lifetimes that can be validated by scientists, such as in the reincarnation cases researched by Ian Stevenson, MD at the University of Virginia. We have also explored spiritual realms as described by clairvoyants Echo Bodine and Judy Goodman, as well as by Ahtun Re, an Egyptian spirit guide who was last incarnate over 3000 years ago, who is channeled through Kevin Ryerson.

I would like to conclude by referring to two cases in which past-life memories were accessed in childhood. One is the case of Anne Frank | Barbro Karlen, which is featured in *Born Again.*

Anne Frank was persecuted as a Jew. In contemporary times, Barbro Karlen, the reincarnation of Anne Frank, was born into a Christian family. Consider that if in the era of World War II, the Nazis knew that one could be born Jewish in one lifetime and Christian in another, then the Holocaust could never have happened. Similarly, if people understood that they could be born Muslim in one lifetime and Jewish or Christian in another, Shiite in one incarnation and Sunni in another, the violence we witness in the Middle East would cease. The Anne Frank | Barbro Karlen case exemplifies the positive societal change that objective evidence of reincarnation can bring about.

Evidence of reincarnation will continue to grow as memories of past incarnations will continue to come out of the mouths of our children. Ian Stevenson, who pioneered scientific research of children who remember past lives, died in 2007. Others, though, continue his work and independently researched cases continue to demonstrate that souls can change religious and ethnic affiliation from one incarnation to another. The second such case that I would like to cite involves a Muslim boy, Kemal Atasoy, who remembered a past lifetime in which he was a Christian.

In a book written by Jim Tucker, MD, of the University of Virginia, entitled *Life Before Life*, Dr. Tucker summaries the work that the late Ian Stevenson performed over the span of 40 years. Dr. Tucker addresses and refutes each argument that a skeptic may raise to try to dismiss Dr. Stevenson's work.

The very first case that Dr. Tucker describes in his book involves Kemal Atasoy, a six-year-old Muslim boy in Turkey who in great detail recalled a lifetime in which he was a wealthy Christian merchant named Karakas who lived in Istanbul, 500 miles from where Kemal was born and raised. Kemal's memories were later validated through meticulous research.

In *Life Before Life,* Dr. Tucker asks, "How did this little boy, living in a town 500 miles away, know so many things about a man who had died in Istanbul fifty years before he was born?...What possible explanation could there be? Kemal had a very simple answer; he said that he had been the man in a previous life."[1]

The next step in human evolution is to realize that we are universal souls that can incarnate in any cultural and religious setting. With this understanding, let us stop violence based on differences in religious, ethnic, national or racial affiliation. Earth is the school that we attend in order to develop and grow so that eventually, we may attain higher levels of the spiritual world and thus become closer to God. Let us stop the destruction of ourselves and the infrastructure of our civilizations based on false and limited identity.

Let me close with an analogy taken from *Return of the Revolutionaries.* Though in an incarnation that occurred 200 years ago, I was known as a revolutionary, I would rather not use that term any longer, for it is associated with conflict. Instead, I would like to be an evolutionary. I hope that you will become an evolutionary too.

The Rivers and Fish

Imagine the great cultural movements and religions of the world as rivers. A prophet or visionary serves as a fountainhead, who initiates a philosophy, a nation or a religion. As followers join the founder, the rivulet grows into a stream. The river then builds and flows across time, across centuries. Supporters contribute to the movement, though works of art, architecture, literature and music, and the river grows more grand and deep.

Imagine that we are like fish that descend from the spiritual world and become immersed in these rivers. In one lifetime, we swim in the River of Moses, in another lifetime, we swim in the River of Jesus Christ, in yet another the River of Mohammed, in another, the River of Buddha, in another, the River of Hinduism, and so on. While one is immersed in a particular river, we tend to completely identify with that cultural stream. We become a Christian, Muslim, Jew, Hindu or Buddhist. We identify with the particular race, ethnicity and nationality that we find ourselves in. We forget that in other lifetimes, we have swum in the other streams too.

For peace to reign on Earth, we must become conscious of the various paths that we traverse and the various identities that we assume. We must remember that from a spiritual perspective, we are the fish, not the rivers. We are universal souls that experience these varied streams. Let us live with this awareness, so that we may all live in peace.

Endnotes

Chapter 5

1. Larry Dossey, *The Power of Premonitions*, Penguin Group, 2009, p.45-49
2. Ibid, p. 46

Chapter 8

1. Joseph Head and S. L. Cranston, *Reincarnation, an East-West Anthology,* The Theosophical Publishing House, 1961, p. 39

Chapter 9

1. Pat Kubis and Mark Macy, *Conversations Beyond the Light: With Departed Friends and Colleagues by Electronic Means*, Griffin Publishing/Continuing Life Research, Boulder, CO USA, 1995, p. 102
2. Ibid, p. 106
3. Ibid, p. 65
4. Ibid, p. 53
5. Ibid, p. 9
6. Ibid, p. 59
7. Ibid, p. 18
8. Ibid, p. 52
9. Ibid, p. 55

Chapter 11

1. Stevenson, Ian: Reincarnation and Biology, A Contribution to the Etiology of Birthmarks and Birth Defects, Volume 2, Praeger, 1997, p. 1937
2. Tucker, Jim B: Life Before Life, St. Martin's Press, 2005, p. 9

3. Schwartz, Gary: The Sacred Promise: How Science is Discovering Spirit's Collaboration with Us in Our Daily Lives, Atria Books/Beyond Words, 2011
4. Dossey, Larry: The Power of Premonitions, Penguin Group, 2009, p. 36
5. Ibid, p. 7
6. Ibid, p. 3
7. Ibid, p. 6
8. Ibid, p. 6
9. Ibid, p. 65
10. Ibid, p. 66
11. Ibid, p. 116
12. Ibid, p. 158
13. Ibid, p. 35, 141
14. Ibid, p. 69

Chapter 14

1. http://en.wikipedia.org/wiki/Amorite
2&3. Jack Kornfield, *The Art of Forgiveness, Lovingkindness, and Peace,* Bantam Books, New York, NY, 2002

Conclusion

1. Jim B. Tucker, *Life Before Life: A Scientific Investigation of Children's Memories of Previous Live,* St. Martin's Press, New York, NY, 2005, p. xiv

Walter Semkiw, MD, MPH

Walter is a medical doctor, having served as a Medical Director of Unocal 76, a Fortune 500 company, and as an Assistant Chief in Occupational Medicine at a major medical center in San Francisco. Walter graduated Phi Beta Kappa from the University of Illinois in Biology. He has a Masters Degree in Public Health.

In addition to *Origin of the Soul and the Purpose of Reincarnation*, Walter is the author of *Return of the Revolutionaries: The Case for Reincarnation and Soul Groups Reunited,* published in the United States, and *Born Again,* published in India, Indonesia, Serbia and the United States.

Walter has founded the Institute for the Integration of Science, Intuition and Spirit, which is dedicated to researching reincarnation, soul evolution and related phenomena scientifically. Our website, www.ReincarnationResearch.com, serves as a resource to study, publish and archive reincarnation cases. www.Reincarnation Research.com also promotes the positive societal transformation that objective evidence of reincarnation can bring.

Walter has been a presenter at the first four meetings of the World Congress for Regression Therapy, held in the Netherlands, India, Brazil and Turkey. He has presented at the Society for Scientific Exploration (SSE), which was cofounded by Ian Stevenson, MD. He has served two terms on the Board of Directors of the International Association for Regression Research and Therapies (IARRT).

Walter has appeared on CNN and has been featured in Newsweek and newsweek.com. He has been cited on numerous occasions in the Times of India, which has the largest circulation of any English language newspaper in the world.

Website and E-mail address for Walter Semkiw, MD:

www.ReincarnationResearch.com
walter@ReincarnationResearch.com

Made in United States
Orlando, FL
22 December 2024

56430043R00104